SCHOLASTIC

100
LITERACY
HOMEWORK

RENEWED PRIMARY FRAMEWORK

100 LITERACY HOMEWORK ACTIVITIES

SCOTTISH PRIMARY 6

YEAR 5

Credits

Author
Chris Webster

Updated by
Stuart Graver

Series consultant
Pam Dowson

Series editor
Tracy Kewley

Development editor
Rachel Mackinnon

Assistant editor
Alex Albrighton

Illustrations
Phil Garner/Beehive Illustration and
Ray and Corinne Burrows

Book layout
Macmillan Publishing Solutions

Mixed Sources
Product group from well-managed
forests and other controlled sources
www.fsc.org Cert no. TT-COC-002769
© 1996 Forest Stewardship Council
FSC

Text © 2001, 2009, Chris Webster
Text © 2009, Stuart Graver
© 2009 Scholastic Ltd

Designed using Adobe InDesign

Published by Scholastic Ltd
Villiers House
Clarendon Avenue
Leamington Spa
Warwickshire CV32 5PR

www.scholastic.co.uk

Printed by Bell and Bain Ltd, Glasgow

1 2 3 4 5 6 7 8 9   9 0 1 2 3 4 5 6 7 8

British Library Cataloguing-in-Publication Data
A catalogue record for this book is available from the British Library.

ISBN 978-1407-10119-4

Acknowledgements
The publishers gratefully acknowledge permission to reproduce the following copyright material:

David Higham Associates for the use of an extract from *Princess by Mistake* by Penelope Liveley © 1993, Penelope Liveley (1993, Hodder Wayland); for the use of an extract from *George's Marvellous Medicine* by Roald Dahl © 1982, Roald Dahl (1982, Jonathan Cape and Penguin Books Ltd); for the use of an extract from *Kensuke's Kingdom* by Michael Morpurgo © 1999, Michael Morpurgo (1999, Egmont) and for the use of an extract from *Robin of Sherwood* by Michael Morpurgo © 1996, Michael Morpurgo (1996, Pavilion Books). **Aidan Gibbons** for the use of stills from the film *The Piano* by Aidan Gibbons © 2007, Aidan Gibbons (2007, Aidan Gibbons). **HarperCollins Publishers** for the use of an extract from *Private Peaceful* by Michael Morpurgo © 2003, Michael Morpurgo (2003, HarperCollins). **HarperCollins Publishers (USA)** for the use of an extract from *Duckula and the ghost train mystery* by John Broadhead © 1988, John Broadhead (1988, Collins). **Hodder Children's Books** for the use of extracts from 'Bre-nancy and the 13 plantains', 'Papa Bois' and 'Toewi and Kroemoe' all from *Stories from the Caribbean* by Petronella Breinburg © 1999, Petronella Breinburg (1999, Wayland). **Macmillan Children's Books** for the use of extracts from *The Story of Robin Hood* retold by Robert Leeson © 1996, Robert Leeson (1996, Kingfisher). **Oxford University Press** for the use of an extract from *The Greeks* by Mark McArthur © 2003, Mark McArthur (2003, Oxford University Press). **Random House Group** for the use of an extract from *The Lottie Project* by Jacqueline Wilson © 1997, Jacqueline Wilson (1997, Doubleday). **The Sharland Organisation** for the use of an extract from *Super Gran Rules OK!* by Forrest Wilson © 1984, Forrest Wilson (1984, Puffin). **The Society of Authors** for the use of an extract from 'The Highwayman' by Alfred Noyes © 1914, Alfred Noyes (1914, O Ditson). **Chris Webster** for the use of 'Stop Animal Testing' from *All new 100 Literacy Hours – Year 5* by Chris Webster © 2005, Chris Webster (2005, Scholastic). **Kit Wright** for the use of 'My Dad, Your Dad' by Kit Wright from *Rabbiting On* by Kit Wright © 1978, Kit Wright (1978, Collins).

Every effort has been made to trace copyright holders for the works reproduced in this book, and the publishers apologise for any inadvertent omissions.

 Contents

CONTENTS

INTRODUCTION

100 Literacy Homework Activities: Year 5

About the series

The *100 Literacy Homework Activities* series provides easy-to-use, photocopiable homework sheets for Key Stage 1 and 2 children. Each book in the series contains 100 homework activities that can be embedded into any school homework programme. Each activity sheet provides instructions for the child and a brief note to the helper, stating simply and clearly its purpose and suggesting support and/or further challenge to offer the child. The activities are clearly linked to the renewed Primary Framework for Literacy and are organised by Block (Narrative, Non-fiction, Poetry), then by Unit.

Core skills activities

At the end of each Unit, you will find a number of 'Core skills' activities, designed to support the development of key literacy skills such as word recognition (Years 1 and 2 only), word structure and spelling, and sentence structure and punctuation. Some of the Core skills activities are linked to the content of the units; others are intended to be used for discrete teaching and can be used at any time.

Teachers' notes

The teachers' notes starting on page 8 provide further information about each activity, with notes on setting the homework, differentiation and follow-up work. The Narrative, Non-fiction and Poetry objectives on the teachers' notes show how activities are linked to the Unit plans, while the reference grid on pages 6 and 7 shows how the objectives from Strands 1 to 12 of the Framework are covered in the book. Links to the Scottish curriculum are provided on the Scholastic website (see page 7).

Using the resources

The best way to use these homework resources is to use them flexibly, integrating them with a series of literacy sessions over a number of days. At primary level, homework should be about 'consolidating and reinforcing skills and understanding, particularly in literacy and numeracy' (Department for Children, Schools and Families: Homework Guidelines). Although the homework sheets can be used to support assessment, their main purpose is to reinforce and extend literacy work carried out in class or to help children prepare for upcoming work.

Supporting your helpers

It is vital that parents or carers understand what you are trying to achieve with homework. As well as the 'Dear helper' notes on each sheet, there is a homework diary on page 5 which can be photocopied and sent home with the homework. Multiple copies of these can be fastened together to make a longer term homework record. Discuss with parents/carers what is meant by 'help'. Legitimate help will include sharing the reading of texts, helping to clarify problems, discussing possible answers and so on, but at some stage the child should be left to do his or her best. Tell parents/carers how much time you expect the child to spend on homework. If, after that time, a child is stuck, or has not finished, they should not be forced to continue. Ask parents/carers to write a brief explanation and say that you will give extra help the next day. If children are succeeding with a task and need more time, this can be allowed – but bear in mind that children need a varied and balanced home life!

Using the activities with *100 Literacy Framework Lessons*

Links have been provided on the teachers' notes for those who wish to use the homework activities with the corresponding *100 Literacy Framework Lessons* book. The teachers' notes show if and where a homework task might fit within the context of the appropriate *100 Literacy Framework Lessons* Unit.

📖 Homework diary

Name of activity and date sent home	Child's comments		Helper's comments	Teacher's comments
	Did you like this activity? Draw a face. 🙂 a lot 😐 a little 🙁 not much	How much did you learn? Draw a face. 🙂 a lot 😐 a little 🙁 not much		

Framework objectives

Objectives	Linked lessons (page numbers)
Strand 1: Speaking	
Tell a story using notes designed to cue techniques, such as repetition, recap and humour.	122
Present a spoken argument, sequencing points logically, defending views with evidence and making use of persuasive language.	70, 80, 81
Use and explore different question types and different ways words are used, including in formal and informal contexts.	80, 82, 92
Strand 2: Listening and responding	
Identify different question types and evaluate their impact on the audience.	88, 92
Identify some aspects of talk that vary between formal and informal occasions.	57, 80, 81, 82, 88
Analyse the use of persuasive language.	70, 81, 100, 101, 102, 103
Strand 3: Group discussion and interaction	
Plan and manage a group task over time using different levels of planning.	
Understand different ways to take the lead and support others in groups.	
Understand the process of decision making.	
Strand 4: Drama	
Reflect on how working in role helps to explore complex issues.	
Perform a scripted scene making use of dramatic conventions.	74, 75
Use and recognise the impact of theatrical effects in drama.	75, 120, 125
Strand 6: Word structure and spelling	
Spell words containing unstressed vowels.	36, 47, 72, 78, 79, 86, 95, 97, 99, 112, 113
Know and use less common prefixes and suffixes, such as *im-, ir, -cian.*	48, 49
Group and classify words according to their spelling patterns and their meanings.	47, 56, 72, 78, 79, 101, 102, 114
Strand 7: Understanding and interpreting texts	
Make notes on and use evidence from across a text to explain events or ideas.	31, 32, 39, 41, 42, 50, 51, 53, 57, 58, 60, 62, 67, 68, 93, 94, 102, 103, 104, 105, 106, 120, 125
Infer writers' perspectives from what is written and from what is implied.	31, 32, 41, 42, 53, 54, 58, 62, 63, 103, 104, 105
Compare different types of narrative and information texts and identify how they are structured.	35, 37, 38, 39, 40, 44, 55, 57, 58, 60, 61, 62, 63, 83, 89, 90, 96, 115, 117, 122, 126
Distinguish between everyday use of words and their subject-specific use.	74
Explore how writers use language for comic and dramatic effects.	44, 56, 101, 102, 118, 123, 127

◼ SCHOLASTIC
www.scholastic.co.uk

Framework objectives

Objectives	Linked lessons (page numbers)
Strand 8: Engaging with and responding to texts	
Reflect on reading habits and preferences and plan personal reading goals.	29, 30, 58, 59
Compare the usefulness of techniques such as visualisation, prediction and empathy in exploring the meaning of texts.	28, 34, 41, 42, 67, 68, 69, 121
Compare how a common theme is presented in poetry, prose and other media.	44
Strand 9: Creating and shaping texts	
Reflect independently and critically on own writing and edit and improve it.	36, 52, 84, 85, 91, 107
Experiment with different narrative forms and styles to write their own stories.	29, 33, 39, 43, 45, 46, 61, 62, 71, 76
Adapt non-narrative forms and styles to write fiction or factual texts, including poems.	52, 59, 84, 85, 107, 108, 109, 110, 111, 116
Vary the pace and develop the viewpoint through the use of direct and reported speech, portrayal of action and selection of detail.	34, 37, 38, 61, 62, 63, 64, 66
Create multi-layered texts, including use of hyperlinks and linked web pages.	85
Strand 10: Text structure and organisation	
Experiment with the order of sections and paragraphs to achieve different effects.	81, 89, 107, 108
Change the order of material within a paragraph, moving the topic sentence.	58, 77, 108
Strand 11: Sentence structure and punctuation	
Adapt sentence construction to different text-types, purposes and readers.	37, 61, 62, 63, 68, 73, 76, 84, 85, 87, 98, 107, 109, 110, 42, 43, 45, 46, 119, 124
Punctuate sentences accurately, including using speech marks and apostrophes.	36, 54, 61, 62, 63, 64, 65, 98, 107, 108
Strand 12: Presentation	
Adapt handwriting for specific purposes, for example, printing, use of italics.	
Use a range of ICT programs to present texts, making informed choices about which electronic tools to use for different purposes.	

Links to the Scottish curriculum can be found at www.scholastic.co.uk/literacyhomework/y5 (click on Free resources)

Narrative – Unit 1 Novels and stories by significant children's authors

Page 28 Setting the scene
Narrative objective: To visualise the setting of stories described in the text.
Setting the homework: Read through the extract discussing the vocabulary and techniques used to help the reader create a picture in their imagination. Encourage the children to share what they see in their imagination.
Differentiation: More confident learners may wish to find another extract of their own to sketch or write their own description of a scene for others to sketch.
Back at school: Look at some of the pictures drawn and discuss the differing versions. Any children who have found a scene or picture and described this in their own words could get a friend to draw it from their description and then compare the result to the original picture.
Link to _100 Literacy Framework Lessons Y5_: NU1, Phase 4: activities linked to _Kensuke's Kingdom_.

Page 29 Beginnings
Narrative objective: To experiment with different types of opening.
Setting the homework: This homework is ideal preparation for story writing as it encourages children to think about what makes a good beginning. Tell the children they will be writing their own story back in school, so it is important to think about what makes them want to read on in a story.
Back at school: Discuss the different beginnings. Ask: _What type are they? What makes you want to read on? What do you think happens next?_ Children should plan their stories soon after this homework. The 'Character cards' on page 33 could also be used to build the children's story.
Link to _100 Literacy Framework Lessons Y5_: NU1, Phase 1: comparing story openings.

Page 30 My favourite author
Narrative objective: To collect information about an author.
Setting the homework: Talk through the different types of information the children need to access and possible additional information they might come across and wish to include. Try to motivate and inspire them to discover lots of information by setting a challenge or mentioning a presentation (see Back at school).
Differentiation: More confident learners may like to explore more than one author or expand on the categories.
Back at school: Invite the children to prepare mini presentations about their author.
Link to _100 Literacy Framework Lessons Y5_: NU1, Phase 3: investigating authors.

Page 31 Phrenological characters
Narrative objective: To make inferences about the author's perspective on a character.
Setting the homework: Explain that phrenology was once thought to be a science. Phrenologists believed that they could read a person's character by reading the bumps on their heads. Ask the children to look at the diagram while you go over some of the more difficult terms, such as _conscientious_.
Differentiation: This is a fun approach to the study of character, so all the children should attempt it. Less confident learners will need help with some of the terms. Definitions of the four or five most difficult words could be written on the back of their sheets.
Back at school: Discuss which bumps the children shaded in to describe the characters. If time allows, a fun follow-up would be to ask the children to try to read each others' characters.
Link to _100 Literacy Framework Lessons Y5_: NU1, Phases 1 and 2: work on characters.

Page 32 Building characters
Narrative objective: To understand the different ways of presenting characters in writing.
Setting the homework: Discuss the different methods of providing information about characters, including action, dialogue and description. If time allows, share some examples from the class story or a text currently being used by the children.
Differentiation: More confident learners could write their own examples to show the three main ways of presenting characters. They may be able to add a fourth way – what the reader infers.
Back at school: Discuss the techniques identified and share any examples.
Link to _100 Literacy Framework Lessons Y5_: NU1, Phase 2: exploring characters in _The Lottie Project_.

Page 33 Character cards
Narrative objective: To note ideas for characters.
Setting the homework: Tell the children that the first step is to decide on a name for each character. Then they should choose two contrasting characters as the basis for detailed character sketches.
Differentiation: Less confident learners could just write one character sketch.
Back at school: Use the characters as the basis for building up a story.

Page 34 Tramp trouble
Narrative objective: To track events from a different character's point of view.
Setting the homework: Explain the task. If time allows, read the passage and discuss how the viewpoint could be changed. Draw children's attention to the guidance notes after the passage.
Differentiation: Less confident learners may be helped by being given a starter – for example, _Tim and Tom_ (or girls' names if preferred) _tried the iron ring on the church door. It turned and the door opened. Tom giggled, but Tim said, "Shh... what's that breathing sound?"_
Back at school: Share and discuss the rewritten stories. Apply the skill to a story that is currently being studied.

Page 35 Time for a break
Narrative objective: To organise a scene using paragraphs effectively.
Setting the homework: Recap on the purpose and use of paragraphs and, if possible, work through an example as a class, paragraphing a block of text. Show the children how to demarcate paragraphs using the symbol //.
Differentiation: All children should be able to do this but less confident learners may require a more structured recap on the use of paragraphs.
Back at school: Invite children to explain how they paragraphed the writing and why, and discuss any differences of opinion.
Link to _100 Literacy Framework Lessons Y5_: NU1, Phase 2: activities linked to _The Lottie Project_.

Page 36 Editing – Core skills
Objective: To edit and improve writing.
Setting the homework: Explain that the notes are to there help. For example, if the note says 'punctuation', there is a punctuation mistake in the line opposite. After editing, the children should produce a neatly written, improved version.
Differentiation: Notes for less confident learners could be simplified – for example, reference to grammatical errors could be dropped.
Back at school: Discuss the errors that the children found and their suggestions for improvement. The most important thing is for them to apply the skill to redrafting a piece of their own work.

Page 37 Which person? – Core skills
Objective: To adapt sentence construction for different purposes.
Setting the homework: Go over the explanation, particularly the conjugation of the verb, *to be*. Note that the past tense has been chosen because this is the usual story-telling tense. This will help the children to see that each person has both singular and plural forms.
Differentiation: Less confident learners should be able to do this exercise in a mechanical way, that is by looking for the words *I* and *you*, though they may not fully grasp the concept of point of view.
Back at school: Identify the viewpoint of each text. When the children next write a story, encourage them to try a viewpoint they have not used very often.

Page 38 Indirect dinosaurs – Core skills
Objective: To understand the difference between direct and reported speech.
Setting the homework: The main point of this homework is the simple recognition of reported speech. Tell children to look for the phrases *says* or *said that*. Point out that reported speech is sometimes indicated by other verbs of speech, such as *told, asked* or *shouted*. There is an example in the text. Reassure the children that there is nothing difficult about direct and reported (or indirect) speech – they use it all the time.
Back at school: Go over the examples of indirect speech.

Narrative – Unit 2 Traditional stories, fables, myths and legends

Page 39 Mercury and the Forester
Narrative objective: To read and analyse features of a text type.
Setting the homework: Explain the differences between myths, legends and fables. A myth explains important things about existence ('Pandora's Box' explains how suffering came into the world); a legend is a story based on events in the past which may or may not be true (King Arthur); a fable is a short story written to prove a moral.
Differentiation: Less confident learners may have difficulty in explaining how the fable is different from an ordinary story. Encourage them to look for obvious things – for example, it is shorter, there is less dialogue, it leads to a moral. More confident learners may prefer to use page 40 'The Mouse and the Lion'.
Back at school: Discuss how the fable is different from an ordinary story. Share examples of the fables leading to the same moral. Read more of Aesop's fables. Make a list of morals and ask the children to choose one and write a fable to go with it.

Page 40 The Mouse and the Lion
Narrative objective: To read and analyse features of the text type.
Setting the homework: Read one of Aesop's fables each day in the week leading up to the homework. Discuss the main structure and ideas of the fables – a simple message/moral and animal focus – so the children have the basic idea of how Aesop's fables are structured.
Differentiation: Challenge more confident learners to produce their own idea for a fable. Less confident learners may prefer to use page 39 'Mercury and the Forester'.
Back at school: Combine ideas to produce a quick outline for a new Aesop's fable.

Page 41 Character thoughts
Narrative objective: To record inferences and demonstrate understanding of characters.
Setting the homework: Read through the extract provided and show how specific phrases can help us to understand a character's thoughts. Together, begin to consider what the character might be thinking.
Back at school: Hold a whole-class discussion and jot down children's ideas to produce a range of possible thoughts.
Link to *100 Literacy Framework Lessons Y5*: NU2, Phase 2: identifying characters' thoughts.

Page 42 The Diary of Robin Hood

Narrative objective: To record inferences and demonstrate understanding of characters by writing in the first person.

Setting the homework: Read through the text to ensure all the children are clear on the task and the character in question. Briefly discuss an example of inference on the reader's part.

Differentiation: Some children will require a run-through of this task.

Back at school: Record the diary entries for others to listen to. These could then be kept for future reference in the reading area/library.

Link to *100 Literacy Framework Lessons Y5*: NU2, Phase 2: identifying characters' thoughts.

Page 43 A tale to tell

Narrative objective: To present an oral retelling of the legend of Robin Hood.

Setting the homework: Discuss the intended audience with the children and give a few solid examples of how to retell for a younger audience focusing on vocabulary, sentence structure and editing.

Differentiation: Less confident learners may need to tell just a section of the story.

Back at school: Read the new versions to younger children or possibly record some for use by other classes in school.

Page 44 The same but different

Narrative objective: To make comparisons between written narratives.

Setting the homework: Consider general stories, TV programmes or films that have been produced or made over and over again. Ask the children if they can think of any examples (for example, Batman and Robin Hood). Engage in a discussion on how any of these versions are similar to or different from each other.

Differentiation: More confident learners may be able to research alternative versions online and extend the comparison to three or more different narratives.

Back at school: List the differences and similarities found and discuss which versions are the children's favourites and why.

Page 45 Arthur: chosen king

Narrative objective: To plan and write a new version of a legend.

Setting the homework: Discuss with the children what they know about the legend of King Arthur. Even today's generation can reconstruct the bare bones of the story. The discussion will serve to show the many different versions of the story. Encourage them to retell the story in any way they like.

Differentiation: Some children may need help with some of the words in the text, such as *engraved, Candlemas, Pentecost, tournament* and *scabbard*.

Back at school: Share the different retellings of the legend.

Link to *100 Literacy Framework Lessons Y5*: NU2, Phase 3: activities linked to the legend of King Arthur.

Page 46 The Lambton Worm

Narrative objective: To plan and write a new version of a legend.

Setting the homework: Explain this is a simple version of 'choice' stories found in books like the 'Fighting Fantasy' series and in computer adventure games. Explain how to read the 'choice' story.

Back at school: Children should use the format to write their 'choice' stories based on myths or legends. Writing in this format reinforces a number of key skills:

- planning with a beginning, main character, series of events and a well-defined ending are essential or the choices will not work
- it gives children experience of writing stories in the present tense
- they can write their story in the second or third person.

Page 47 Full to -ful – Core skills
Objective: To group and classify words according to their spelling patterns and their meanings.
Setting the homework: Revise the terms 'noun' and 'adjective'. Warn children to watch out for words ending in 'y'.
Differentiation: All the children should be able to do this homework.
Back at school: Monitor the application of this rule in the children's writing.

Page 48 What do you do? – Core skills
Objective: To know and use less common prefixes and suffixes.
Setting the homework: Go over the explanation on the sheet and explain what to write under the pictures.
Differentiation: Less confident learners could cut the pictures out to make cards which the helper can use as flash cards. The child can say the '-cian' words before writing them.
Back at school: Go over the pictures and check that all the children know how to form and spell the '-cian' words.

Page 49 Opposites by prefix – Core skills
Objective: To know and use less common prefixes and suffixes.
Setting the homework: It is important that the children understand that each word has a specific prefix. These will not work on a 'pick and mix' basis.
Differentiation: Many of the opposites are quite difficult words both in spelling and meaning. Less confident learners could be giving lists of simpler antonyms to match together.
Back at school: Write in the correct prefixes as the children suggest them.

Narrative – Unit 3 Stories from other cultures

Page 50 Stories from around the world
Narrative objective: To explore how literature provides us with important cultural information.
Setting the homework: Provide a few clear examples of different books that reflect different cultures. Refer to films and TV programmes as appropriate. Suggest ways that the children might find out the information required.
Differentiation: All children should be able to access this activity but less confident children may need to be shown the clues that convey the information required.
Back at school: Collect examples of cultural literature together as a reference for the class.

Page 51 Spot the difference
Narrative objective: To identify cultural differences with reference to a text.
Setting the homework: Read through the texts and highlight a few obvious sections that will provide a starting point for the children. Challenge them to find more.
Differentiation: All children should be able to find literal clues but more confident learners should look to see what can be inferred from the text.
Back at school: Discuss the children's findings and, for each passage, find the top three clues.

Page 52 Culture clues
Narrative objective: To consider the use of language as a technique to portray a cultural difference.
Setting the homework: Discuss what types of things the children could include in their text.
Differentiation: All children should be able to access this task although some may wish to produce more than others.
Back at school: Compare and share the children's work and allow them to evaluate the effectiveness of each of their efforts.

Page 53 A different point of view

Narrative objective: To explore a story from different characters' points of view.

Setting the homework: Use the thought bubble method to focus the children on different characters' feelings. Read through the text and ensure all children are clear on which character(s) they are to focus on.

Differentiation: More confident learners could look at a number of characters within the same scene.

Back at school: Collate the children's ideas to produce thought bubbles for each of the different characters. These could be used to create a display.

Link to *100 Literacy Framework Lessons Y5*: NU3, Phases 1 and 3: activities linked to *Bre-nancy and the 13 Plantains*.

Page 54 A letter to...

Narrative objective: To write in the role of a particular character.

Setting the homework: Emphasise that when writing a letter in role as a character, it is not just what is said but *how* it is said that is important. Provide and share examples that look at style of speech, character traits and content.

Differentiation: Limit the context for less confident learners and expand the ideas for the more confident.

Back at school: Share the children's work and ideas, and identify key traits of the chosen characters.

Page 55 Caribbean folk tale

Narrative objective: To explore the difference between oral and written narrative.

Setting the homework: Explain to the children that they must never think that spoken language is inferior to written language because it contains hesitations and repetitions. In the history of humankind, spoken language came first and in our personal histories and lives, spoken language comes first. Use the explanation to explain the differences between spoken and written language.

Differentiation: Less confident learners could omit the written task.

Back at school: Highlight examples of the differences between spoken and written language as the children feed back. Hold an oral story-telling session in which the children relate their stories and anecdotes.

Page 56 Don't take it literally – Core skills

Objective: To explore how writers use language for effects.

Setting the homework: Explain the difference between 'literal' and 'figurative'.

Differentiation: Children who cannot recognise and understand similes should do more work on them before going on to this stage.

Back at school: Share and discuss children's examples of literal and figurative language.

Page 57 Linstead Market – Core skills

Objective: To explore accent and dialect.

Setting the homework: Explain that they will be reading a traditional Caribbean poem, written in the local dialect. Go over the terms 'accent' and 'dialect' as explained on the sheet. Encourage them to read the poem through once, before re-reading it to do the activity.

Differentiation: Even if the children cannot figure out what some of the dialect words mean, they should be able to distinguish them from words that are just pronounced differently.

Back at school: Discuss differences of accent and dialect in the poem.
- Accent: *me* (my), *wut* (would), *Lard* (Lord), *wat* (what), *Satiday* (Saturday), *an* (and), *marnin'* (morning), *brukfas'* (breakfast), *gran'* (grand), *de* (the), *linga* (linger), *mumma* (mothers), *fe weh* (far away).
- Dialect: *ackee* (fruit), *go a* (to), *quatty* (thing), *not a bite* (not one customer bought anything), *come* (comes), *feel/squeeze up* (feels/squeezes the fruit), *mek me* (I have to), *dem 'tan* (those tangerines), *buy yu* (do you want to buy?), *nyam* (taste), *pickney* (children), *no bring* (won't take).

Narrative – Unit 4 Older literature

Page 58 The Secret Garden
Narrative objective: To explore older literature and read the extract aloud.
Setting the homework: Explain that the extract is the opening to the famous novel, *The Secret Garden*, first published in 1911. Ask the children if any of them have seen the story on television. Encourage them to read the passage aloud. It is written in long, complex sentences which will be more easily accessible if read aloud.
Differentiation: Helpers of less confident learners should first read the passage to their child and then re-read it with the child following or sharing the read.
Back at school: Discuss the character of Mary and the words and phrases the children have picked out. If some of the children have seen a televised version, ask them to say whether the description of Mary matches the character on TV.
Link to *100 Literacy Framework Lessons Y5*: NU1, Phase 1: work on clauses in sentences.

Page 59 Shakespeare's language
Narrative objective: To explore older literature and read the extract aloud.
Setting the homework: Explain that the important thing is to read the text aloud. Shakespeare wrote these words to be performed, not to be read silently. Encourage the children to go further than substituting the glossary notes for the words in italics. They should also simplify the sentence construction.
Differentiation: Less confident learners should make a direct substitution of the glossary notes for the words in italics. You could prepare a version of the sheet in which this has already been done.
Back at school: Ask some of the more confident learners to perform the scene.

Page 60 Treasure Island
Narrative objective: To widen experience of older literature and identify aspects specific to this style.
Setting the homework: Discuss the extract and encourage the children to look for examples that tell us the story is taken from older literature – references to objects, people, time and vocabulary.
Differentiation: Ask less confident children just to highlight evidence from the text only.
Back at school: Find other examples of older/classic literature for the class display.

Page 61 The Jungle Book
Narrative objective: To understand the ideas within a text and rewrite for a modern audience.
Setting the homework: The key idea here is to ensure the children understand that the message or story must be maintained but the speech or language and style can be adjusted.
Differentiation: Adjust the amount of text you wish children to rewrite according to their abilities.
Back at school: Collect the new versions and put into the class reading corner/library for all to share and compare.

Page 62 Desert island

Narrative objective: To write in the style of an author.

Setting the homework: Ask the children to note the date when Robinson Crusoe was first published – it is more than 100 years older than most other classics that they have read! They will notice at once the strangeness of the language, though such is Defoe's direct style, it is rarely a barrier to understanding. Emphasise that they should make up their own adventures for Robinson Crusoe.

Differentiation: Less confident learners could be given the same extract from a retold version of the story. They will miss out on Defoe's language but will still be able to explore character and situation.

Back at school: Share the continuations and discuss how they might fit together to make a new, long Robinson Crusoe story. One possible follow-up would be to write that story, possibly in collaborative groups, each child writing a chapter to an agreed plan.

Link to *100 Literacy Framework Lessons Y5*: NU4, Phase 3: writing in the style of an author.

Page 63 In the style of...

Narrative objective: To write in the style of a particular author.

Setting the homework: Ideally, read one of Robert Louis Stevenson's works as a class story. Emphasise some of the author's main traits as you set the homework – for example, formal style, use of the first person and longish sentences with clauses. Discuss some of the possibilities that the children could go on to write about.

Differentiation: All children should be able to do this activity but less confident children could produce a spoken version.

Back at school: Share excerpts of the children's work or listen to some of the spoken versions.

Link to *100 Literacy Framework Lessons Y5*: NU4, Phase 3: writing in the style of an author.

Page 64 Direct and reported – Core skills

Objective: To use direct and reported speech.

Setting the homework: Go over the explanation on the sheet.

Differentiation: This is a more academic study of direct and reported speech and involves applying rules to change from one to the other. Children should be able to do the activity on page 38 'Indirect dinosaurs' before they attempt this one. Also, any children who do not understand the terms 'clause', 'tense' and 'personal pronoun', will not be able to understand the rules and should work on those terms instead.

Back at school: Go over the answers to the two sets of sentences orally, while the children mark their own work.

Page 65 Old new school – Core skills

Objective: To punctuate sentences accurately.

Setting the homework: Show the children some examples of how speech is set out in real stories.

Differentiation: Children must be confident about punctuating speech before they can tackle this step. Otherwise, there will be so much detail to remember they are likely to get confused. Children who are not ready for this sheet should be given a task for a previous step, such as adding speech marks to dialogue.

Back at school: Apply the skill in writing stories with dialogue. There is a lot to remember when writing dialogue, so do not despair if it takes the children a while to remember it all.

Narrative – Unit 5 Film narrative

Page 66 The Piano: setting
Narrative objective: To explore approaches used to create moods.
Setting the homework: Watch the film from the National Strategies Website. Discuss the words provided on the homework sheet, perhaps asking the children to suggest objects for one example.
Differentiation: All children should be able to access this activity and take it as far as they wish.
Back at school: Share children's ideas and take a class vote on the most popular image for each scene.
Link to *100 Literacy Framework Lessons Y5*: NU5, Phase 1: exploring film techniques; activities linked to *The Piano*.

Page 67 The Piano: characters
Narrative objective: To explore characters in depth.
Setting the homework: Show the children how to complete the task by using another character that the children know well and asking them to suggest words to include inside thought bubbles for the character.
Differentiation: Differentiation will mainly be by outcome but encourage more confident learners to consider inference.
Back at school: Invite children to share their ideas and encourage other children to give constructive feedback.
Link to *100 Literacy Framework Lessons Y5*: NU5, Phase 2: characterisation in *The Piano*.

Page 68 The Piano: relationships
Narrative objective: To demonstrate an understanding of characters by writing a short conversation.
Setting the homework: Use a brief role-play activity to get the children thinking about what characters might say. Recap on dialogue conventions and structure.
Differentiation: More confident learners could attempt to create a dialogue between three or more characters.
Back at school: Act out the different dialogues that children produce and award Oscars!
Link to *100 Literacy Framework Lessons Y5*: NU5, Phase 2: characterisation in *The Piano*.

Page 69 Camera angles
Narrative objective: To understand how camera angles assist with the narrative.
Setting the homework: Children will each need a viewfinder (a small card with a window cut out) for this activity. Use the viewfinder to demonstrate camera angles and discuss reasons for their use. Watch a short excerpt of a film/TV programme and spot close-ups, panning away, zooms, distance shots and so on. Discuss how and why they have been used.
Back at school: Explore alternative shots and angles with a viewfinder.
Link to *100 Literacy Framework Lessons Y5*: NU5, Phase 3: work on camera angles.

Page 70 Dialogue
Narrative objective: To summarise the narrative with a voice-over.
Setting the homework: Play some voice-overs or film blurbs from the start of DVDs so children can hear the techniques used.
Differentiation: Less confident children should be asked to create a shorter voice-over.
Back at school: Compare the children's voice-overs. Give them time to practise then perform their work. If time allows, use ICT to add accompanying music.

Page 71 Lights, camera, action!
Narrative objective: To develop a storyboard for a narrative.
Setting the homework: Do a class storyboard together discussing the key elements to include.
Differentiation: Less confident children may require you to give them a story rather than design one themselves.
Back at school: Display all the children's ideas and vote for a top three. Arrange the children into groups to prepare performances of the top three narratives.
Link to *100 Literacy Framework Lessons Y5*: NU5, Phase 3: creating storyboards for narrative.

Page 72 Except after c – Core skills
Objective: To group and classify words according to their spelling patterns.
Setting the homework: Go over the explanation.
Differentiation: This is a basic spelling rule that all children should learn.
Back at school: Write in the correct spellings in the gaps. Monitor the application of this rule in the children's writing.

Page 73 Are we agreed? – Core skills
Objective: To explore sentence construction and the agreement between nouns and verbs.
Setting the homework: Go over the explanation, placing particular emphasis on the tip at the end. Most people make mistakes about the agreement of noun and verb because the noun is expressed in such a way that it sounds plural.
Differentiation: In order to benefit from this sheet, the children need to understand the terms 'noun', 'verb', 'singular' and 'plural'. Children who have not mastered any of these should be given appropriate consolidation work.
Back at school: Go through the sheet with the children who did the homework. Monitor future work for problems of agreement.

Narrative – Unit 6 Dramatic conventions

Page 74 Computer kids
Narrative objective: To analyse the features of playscripts.
Setting the homework: Explain to the children that the purpose of the task is to focus on the different conventions of scriptwriting. Emphasise that they should first read and enjoy the play scene with their helper.
Differentiation: The problem for less confident children might be in applying all the conventions to an actual script. Put them in small groups and make the scriptwriting a group task.
Back at school: Soon after the homework, the children should apply the conventions to their playscripts, keeping the highlighted homework page in front of them as a model.

Page 75 A mummers' play
Narrative objective: To perform playscripts.
Setting the homework: If possible, enlarge the sheet to A3 to make annotation easier. Explain that this is a scene from a traditional mummers' play. Read the short introduction with the children, and explain that the task is to think about how the play could be performed. The children should annotate the sheet with notes.
Back at school: Ask for a group of volunteers to present the play. Allow ten minutes for preparation, then ask the children to perform. The performances and improvisations could be further polished and performed to a wider audience, such as another class or in a school assembly.

Page 76 Bedtime blues
Narrative objective: To write own playscripts.
Setting the homework: Use page 74 'Computer kids' to remind the children of the conventions used in playscripts. Ideally, the children should take that page home along with this page. Explain that many scripts contain notes explaining how to stage the scene most effectively. This is the purpose of the second part of the activity.
Differentiation: Less confident learners should focus on the first part of the activity.
Back at school: Ensure the children apply the skill to writing their playscripts.

Page 77 Sickly soup – Core skills
Objective: To change the order of material within a paragraph.
Setting the homework: Go over the examples, placing particular emphasis on the effect of re-ordering the sentences.
Differentiation: Most children should be able to do this sheet successfully, providing they understand the explanation. Those who cannot probably need more work on writing correct simple sentences.
Back at school: Invite the children to share their re-ordered sentences. Ask the class to comment on the effect of each one: Ask: *Does the sentence make sense? What is the emphasis of the sentence? Have pronouns been used or changed appropriately?*

Page 78 Verb to noun – Core skills
Objective: To group and classify words according to meaning and spelling.
Setting the homework: Go over the explanation and example on the sheet.
Differentiation: Encourage more confident learners to use some of the pairs of words in sentences.
Back at school: Ask selected children to share sentences.

Page 79 Noun to verb – Core skills
Objective: To group and classify words according to meaning and spelling.
Setting the homework: Go over the explanation and example.
Differentiation: Encourage more confident learners to use some of the pairs of words in sentences.
Back at school: Ask selected children who made sentences to share them.

Non-fiction – Unit 1 Instructions

Page 80 Drawing instructions
Non-fiction objective: To give verbal instructions.
Setting the homework: Provide some examples of clear instructions similar to that required in the homework. It would be useful for children to have experience of drawing while listening to good and bad examples of oral instructions. This could be done through a short game in the days leading up to the homework.
Differentiation: More confident learners should be encouraged to be more adventurous in the detail and extent of their drawings.
Back at school: Invite the children to report back on how successful they were and to try out their instructions for their own drawings on others. Assess the accuracy and extent of the instructions together.
Link to *100 Literacy Framework Lessons Y5*: NFU1, Phases 1 and 2: giving instructions.

Page 81 Helpline!
Non-fiction objective: To practise verbal instructions in a help-desk simulation.
Setting the homework: Invite volunteers to try the homework task in front of the class, with no preparation. Having seen several attempts, the children will understand the important elements when doing the homework. Emphasise the importance of extracting information from the caller to enable them to give the best advice. A joint checklist of tips and questions could be created consisting of name, age, main problem, tips and so on.
Back at school: Use role play again to see how the homework has developed the children's ideas.

Page 82 Video phone

Non-fiction objective: To read and investigate instructions.
Setting the homework: Encourage the children to read the instructions carefully and then act out making a call. While doing this, an adult should check that they are carrying out the instructions correctly.
Differentiation: Explain to less confident learners that *imperative* simply means 'something you must do'. Thus, if you do not follow one of the instructions, your call will not get through. Ask them to underline the words that say what you must do.
Back at school: Share the instructions the children have written and use them to collect more examples of imperative verbs.

Page 83 Instructions test drive

Non-fiction objective: To evaluate a set of instructions.
Setting the homework: Follow the set of instructions and begin to verbally evaluate these together.
Differentiation: Ask less confident children to complete the first task only — commenting on the written instructions.
Back at school: Share the children's ideas to produce the definitive set of instructions for brushing teeth.
Link to *100 Literacy Framework Lessons Y5*: NFU1, Phase 3: writing instructions.

Page 84 Paper planes

Non-fiction objective: To write a set of instructions and edit for clarity and correctness.
Setting the homework: Go through the task with the children and do the first couple of possible instructions together. Emphasise the possibility of using bullet points, diagrams and so on.
Differentiation: More confident learners could write different sets of instructions to assess which is more effective and why.
Back at school: Share the children's findings and produce a class list of tips and reminders for writing instructions.
Link to *100 Literacy Framework Lessons Y5*: NFU1, Phase 3: analysing instructions.

Page 85 Fun and games

Non-fiction objective: To create a plan for a multi-layered text.
Setting the homework: Show the children some good examples of multi-layered texts in the classroom. Focus on how the layers are created and why. Suggest the reasons for and appropriate use of 'links' within these kinds of texts. Remind the children of the importance of writing clear instructions, and of using diagrams and bullets where appropriate.
Differentiation: Provide alternative games with differing levels of complexity.
Back at school: Discuss and compare the children's layouts. Allow the children to create their text in ICT, incorporating any improvements from class discussions.
Link to *100 Literacy Framework Lessons Y5*: NFU1, Phase 3: writing instructions.

Page 86 Look, Cover, Write, Check (1) – Core skills

Objective: To spell words containing unstressed vowels.
Setting the homework: Show the children how to use the Look, Cover, Write, Check method of learning unusual spellings. Give them time to add their individual spellings to the list.
Differentiation: The list is the first part of 100 commonly misspelled words for this age group. Words in the list should be adjusted for the most and least confident learners. The most important way to differentiate is to ensure that the children add their own words.
Back at school: Reinforce learning by asking the children to test each other in pairs. Emphasise the fun rather than the test element.

Page 87 All in a good clause (1) – Core skills
Objective: To adapt sentence construction to different types, purposes and readers.
Setting the homework: Revise necessary terminology – 'adjective', 'clause' – and introduce the term 'relative pronoun'. Relative pronouns relate one clause to another.
Differentiation: Though less confident learners may well be mystified by the terminology, they should have no difficulty filling the gaps by using their innate sense of 'what sounds right'.
Back at school: Go over the gap-filling exercise. Give further practice on expanding sentences with adjective clauses.

Non-fiction – Unit 2 Recounts

Page 88 TV talk
Non-fiction objective: To evaluate the effectiveness of an interview.
Setting the homework: Watch or listen to an interview as this will focus the children on the structure of interviews and the techniques used by interviewers. List together the key elements that will ensure a successful interview.
Differentiation: Encourage less confident learners to focus on the features of interviews by asking them to complete the first five sections of the table only.
Back at school: Produce a class guide to interview success.
Link to *100 Literacy Framework Lessons Y5*: NFU2, Phase 1: work on interview techniques.

Page 89 Order please!
Non-fiction objective: To revisit the features of a recount text.
Setting the homework: Read the text and be clear on what the children will need to do to re-order the text.
Differentiation: Provide shorter or longer extracts for more or less confident learners.
Back at school: Encourage the children to discuss their recount texts with talk partners.

Page 90 Lusitania recount
Non-fiction objective: To identify common features of recount texts.
Setting the homework: Go over the task, making sure that the children understand each of the terms mentioned at the top of the page.
Differentiation: More confident learners should complete the extension task.
Back at school: Revise the features of recount texts. Go through an enlarged version of the homework text together and ask the children to volunteer to mark it up using different coloured pens.

Page 91 Said
Non-fiction objective: To revise the use of reported speech.
Setting the homework: Highlight the need for alternatives to *said* in general, but especially in recount writing by reading a text where *said* is used continually. Begin to develop a bank of alternatives and set this as a challenge. Emphasise that the task is not about coming up with the most but rather the best alternatives.
Back at school: Collect 'wow' words for *said* and store them as a bank on display.

Page 92 The hot-seat
Non-fiction objective: To collect information using an interview technique and feed this back to a group.
Setting the homework: Model an interview with a volunteer and, if time allows, set up a few practice interviews – talk partners could be used for this. This will help to clarify the key structure and information that each interview will need.
Back at school: Allow time for the children to interview each other on mini topics using what they have learned from the homework.

■ **SCHOLASTIC**
www.scholastic.co.uk

Page 93 Newfoundland notes
Non-fiction objective: To make notes for writing.
Setting the homework: Explain that the purpose of the table is to ensure that the children do not write full sentences when note-making. The table format is used to make children focus on key words and numbers only.
Differentiation: Less confident learners might find it easier if they highlighted key words and numbers before filling in the table.
Back at school: Apply the skill to a real research context.

Page 94 Abbreviations
Non-fiction objective: To use abbreviations in note making.
Setting the homework: Explain the purpose of abbreviations. Full stops are used to indicate abbreviations but commonly used abbreviations usually omit full stops. (American English and older British English use full stops after Dr., Mr., and so on.)
Differentiation: All the children should be able to do this homework.
Back at school: Monitor the children's use of abbreviations in context, ensuring that they are appropriate and correctly punctuated.

Page 95 Beautiful – Core skills
Objective: To spell words containing unstressed vowels.
Setting the homework: Use this sheet as a follow-up to a lesson or part of a lesson on spelling or with any text that contains several examples. Go over the explanation and the first example in the table.
Differentiation: This is a basic spelling rule that all children should learn. If necessary, provide appropriate catch-up work.
Back at school: Use an enlarged version of the sheet to write in the correct spellings in column three as children read them out – or ask the children to write them in. Monitor the application of this rule in children's writing.

Page 96 Hallucinate – Core skills
Objective: To use different types of information texts and identify how they are structured.
Setting the homework: This homework requires a dictionary. To ensure that no child is disadvantaged because they do not have one at home, give each child a dictionary along with the homework sheet.
Differentiation: You may wish to adapt the questions for some children, perhaps by limiting their search to only one or two dictionary features (for example, meaning and part of speech).
Back at school: Discuss the children's answers to the questions. Ask: *Did all the dictionaries give the same information?* If not, discuss the importance of choosing suitable dictionaries for the task.

Page 97 Look, Cover, Write, Check (2) – Core skills
Objective: To spell words containing unstressed vowels.
Setting the homework: Remind the children how to use the Look, Cover, Write, Check method of learning spellings. Give the children time to add their individual spellings to the list.
Differentiation: The list is the second part of 100 commonly misspelled words for this age group. Words included should be adjusted for the most and least confident. Ensure that they add their words to the list.
Back at school: Reinforce learning by asking the children to test each other.

Page 98 Trudy's dream present – Core skills

Objective: To revise the function of pronouns.

Setting the homework: This homework encourages the children to look at the way sentences are related and thus avoid unnecessary repetition of nouns or overuse of pronouns. Write this short paragraph on the board: *Trudy is a pupil at St Mark's Primary School. Trudy is ten. Trudy has lots of friends.* Explain that these three sentences are correct, but don't 'hang together' to form a paragraph. Change Trudy in the second two sentences to *she*, and explain how the *she* refers back to the proper noun *Trudy* and makes the three sentences into one paragraph. Explain that *she* is a pronoun. Revise the definition of 'pronoun' and give examples.

Differentiation: Even children who get confused over the terms 'noun' and 'pronoun' can do the written task.

Back at school: Read examples of the task and discuss which has the best balance of repeated nouns and personal pronouns.

Page 99 Achievement – Core skills

Objective: To spell words containing unstressed vowels.

Setting the homework: Go over the explanation and the first example in the table.

Differentiation: This is a basic spelling rule that all children should learn. If necessary, provide appropriate catch-up work.

Back at school: Use an enlarged version to write in the correct spellings in column three as children read them out – or ask the children to write them in. Monitor the application of this rule in the children's writing.

Non-fiction – Unit 3 Persuasive writing

Page 100 Investigating adverts

Non-fiction objective: To identify key features of persuasive texts.

Setting the homework: Look at an example of persuasive text and summarise the key features – for example, use of imagery, usually written in present tense, emotive language and so on. Challenge the children to look carefully at the text you have chosen to find a feature that no one else does.

Back at school: Ask the children to discuss with their talk partners the most important elements of persuasive writing, and then feed back their ideas to the class.

Page 101 Wow words

Non-fiction objective: To collect and assess the effectiveness of persuasive words and phrases.

Setting the homework: Read through an advert and ask the children to put up their hands when they hear a 'wow' word – a word or phrase that they find very persuasive.

Differentiation: Set different targets for the number of words to be collected according to ability.

Back at school: Collect and display some 'wow' words for persuasive texts.

Link to *100 Literacy Framework Lessons Y5*: NFU3, Phase 2: exploring persuasive language.

Page 102 What persuades us?

Non-fiction objective: To identify different techniques used by writers to persuade.

Setting the homework: Ask the children to discuss the extract with their talk partners.

Differentiation: Ask more confident learners to give their own examples on the same topic.

Back at school: Have a mini debate using the techniques discussed.

Link to *100 Literacy Framework Lessons Y5*: NFU3, Phase 2: exploring persuasive devices; activities linked to the text 'Stop Animal Testing'.

Page 103 One-kid crime wave
Non-fiction objective: To collect and investigate use of persuasive devices.
Setting the homework: The article contains good examples of persuasive devices. Go over the list so that the children understand what they are looking for.
Differentiation: Less confident learners may need help to identify persuasive devices. More confident learners should continue research into persuasive devices by looking at persuasive articles in newspapers and magazines.
Back at school: Collect from the children the persuasive devices they found.
Link to *100 Literacy Framework Lessons Y5*: NFU3, Phase 2: exploring persuasive devices.

Page 104 Fact or opinion? (1)
Non-fiction objective: To understand and identify fact, opinion and bias.
Setting the homework: Give a few good examples of fact, opinion and bias and discuss how we distinguish these. Focus especially on bias and how it can be identified.
Differentiation: You may wish to omit bias for less confident learners. More confident learners may be able to make up their own examples.
Back at school: Hold a 'Fact, opinion and bias quiz'. Teams should think of statements for the others to categorise.

Page 105 Fact or opinion? (2)
Non-fiction objective: To identify fact and opinion in a persuasive text.
Setting the homework: Read the extract aloud and talk to the children about what is being said in this text. Open up the discussion to see which parts the children consider to be fact and which opinion.
Differentiation: Encourage more confident learners to justify their reasoning.
Back at school: Return to the initial text and discuss it in more depth, concentrating on the parts that children found most difficult to classify.
Link to *100 Literacy Framework Lessons Y5*: NFU3, Phase 2: activities linked to the text 'Come to Greece!'.

Page 106 Old school fields
Non-fiction objective: To consider bias and how opinion can be disguised as fact.
Setting the homework: Explain that the letter is typical of many persuasive letters that deliberately distort the truth in order to make a point. The task is to compare the statements in Mr Rudge's letter with the facts as shown on the plan. The reply from the council will be most effective if it politely answers Mr Rudge's points with reference to the facts.
Differentiation: Less confident learners may need help to see how Mr Rudge has distorted facts. This can be done by asking the helper to compare the statements in the letter with the plan.
Back at school: Discuss Mr Rudge's letter. Ask: *Does he really have any grounds at all for complaint?* Share and discuss different letters of reply.

Page 107 Dear Councillor...
Non-fiction objective: To draft a letter for a real purpose.
Setting the homework: Recap on letter structure and features and emphasise that the reason for this particular letter is persuasion. Go through an example plan that children can use as a basis for their homework.
Differentiation: Adjust the number of elements you wish children to address.
Back at school: Invite children to read out their letters and encourage others to give positive feedback.
Link to *100 Literacy Framework Lessons Y5*: NFU3, Phase 2: persuasive letter writing.

Page 108 Read all about it!
Non-fiction objective: To produce an editorial giving a personal viewpoint.
Setting the homework: Read some examples of editorials and then move on to talk the children through the plan, focusing on the key points that need to be included. Give the children a topical news item, national or local, to focus on.
Differentiation: Ask less confident learners to write their editorial as a list of bullet points.
Back at school: Collate the children's editorials into a book for the reading corner/library entitled *Read all about it!*

Page 109 Book advertisement
Non-fiction objective: To draft a persuasive text.
Setting the homework: Discuss the illustration and blurb on the cover of the book which the children are going to advertise (or, if they are all different, discuss a good example). How does the book cover appeal to the reader? How does the blurb get the reader interested? Explain that they will be doing very similar things in their book advertisement, but must not simply copy the cover.
Back at school: Display the finished advertisements around the classroom. Allow ten minutes browsing time, then discuss them: Which ones most catch the attention and why? Do any miss out essential information?

Page 110 Boreham Supertram
Non-fiction objective: To evaluate a text and draft a persuasive letter.
Setting the homework: Explain that the children can use the information about the Boreham Supertram, or write about a real local issue. The important thing is that they carefully follow the format provided and write a series of well-presented arguments.
Differentiation: Less confident learners might concentrate on either setting out a business letter, or writing an argument for or against an issue.
Back at school: Hold a debate about the Boreham Supertram so that the children can air their arguments. Mark the setting out of all the letters after the lesson.

Page 111 Uniform arguments
Non-fiction objective: To construct an argument in note form.
Setting the homework: Explain that half the battle of persuasive writing is thinking of good arguments. It is, therefore, a good idea to jot down all the arguments in note form first. Ask the children to use the arguments for school uniform to help them to think of arguments against.
Differentiation: None needed at this stage. Less confident learners can often argue verbally quite well. It is when it comes to putting their arguments down in writing that support is needed.
Back at school: Use the notes as the basis for a class debate or discussion. This could be followed with a written task. Less confident learners could write up one side of the argument as a short essay, whereas more confident learners could write a balanced essay in which they consider both sides of the argument and then reach a conclusion.
Link to *100 Literacy Framework Lessons Y5*: NFU3, Phase 3: drafting written arguments.

Page 112 Look, Cover, Write, Check (3) – Core skills
Objective: To spell words containing unstressed vowels.
Setting the homework: Remind the children how to use the Look, Cover, Write, Check method of learning spellings. Give them time to add their spellings. Additional blank pages in the same format could be added for children's words.
Differentiation: The list is the third part of 100 commonly misspelled words for this age group. Words included should be adjusted for the most and least confident. However, the most important way to differentiate is to ensure that children add their own words.
Back at school: Reinforce learning by asking the children to test each other in pairs. Emphasise the fun rather than the test element.

Page 113 Adjective to adverb – Core skills
Objective: To spell words containing unstressed vowels.
Setting the homework: Go over the explanation and example.
Differentiation: You may wish to limit the number of words for less confident learners. Encourage more confident learners to use some of the pairs of words in sentences to show they understand the different uses of adjectives and adverbs.
Back at school: Display an enlarged version of the sheet and write in the correct adverbs. Ask selected children, who made up sentences with the words, to share them.

Page 114 From bad to worse – Core skills
Objective: To group and classify words according to their meanings and spellings.
Setting the homework: Go over the explanation and examples.
Differentiation: This activity should be within the capability of most children. More confident learners should be encouraged to use the comparative forms in sentences.
Back at school: Display an enlarged version of the sheet and write in the correct comparative forms. Ask children who made up sentences with the words to share them.

Poetry – Unit 1 Poetic style

Page 115 Poetry analyser
Poetry objective: To explore the elements and features of poetry.
Setting the homework: The children should be given a poem to write about. The poem could be read and discussed. If possible, enlarge the sheet to A3 so that children have more space in which to write. This sheet could also be used for Poetry Unit 2 with page 123 'Meg Merrilies'.
Differentiation: More confident learners should use the headings as guides and write in paragraphs on a separate sheet of paper. Less confident learners may need to leave out all or part of the section on form.
Back at school: Use the responses as a focus for a discussion of the poem.
Link to *100 Literacy Framework Lessons Y5*: PU1, Phases 1 and 2: analysing the language and structure of poetry.

Page 116 The poetry processor
Poetry objective: To write a free verse poem.
Setting the homework: Explain to the children how to use the cards. Emphasise that the poetry processor works best if they respond quickly to the prompt.
Differentiation: Less confident learners may need help with some technical terms, such as 'adjective', 'adverb', 'verb', 'simile'. Definitions could be written on a separate sheet. For the least confident, cards containing these terms should be omitted.
Back at school: Give an opportunity for the children to share their poems. If time allows, develop them further.
Link to *100 Literacy Framework Lessons Y5*: PU1, Phase 3: writing poetry.

Page 117 All kinds of poems
Poetry objective: To explore form in poetry.
Setting the homework: Explain that the task is to match the poems to the definitions. Emphasise how important it is to read and enjoy the poems first!
Differentiation: Spend a few minutes with less confident learners revising the terms 'syllable', 'rhyme' and 'rhythm'.
Back at school: Check that the children have correctly matched the names of the forms to the poems. Read each poem and discuss how the form chosen for each one is suited to its subject matter – the bouncy rhythm of the limerick emphasises humour; the brevity of the haiku emphasises its focused thought; the long lines of the sonnet are appropriate to the solemnity of the subject; the two couplets of the clerihew are appropriate to its simplicity; the rhythm and rhyme of ballad form help the story to flow.

Page 118 Table-top planet

Poetry objective: To explore language effects in poetry.

Setting the homework: Make sure that the children understand the terms 'literal' (realistic, factual) and 'figurative' (imaginative, symbolic). Read the example to the children and discuss how the author has taken a simple object and looked at it in an imaginative way.

Differentiation: All the children should be able to do this activity.

Back at school: Share examples of the literal-figurative poems.

Page 119 All in a good clause (2) – Core skills

Objective: To revise the use of clauses in sentence construction.

Setting the homework: Revise necessary terminology – 'adverb', 'clause', 'subordinate clause', 'conjunction'. Add that there are two types of conjunctions:

- coordinating, which join clauses with equal weight. The commonest coordinating conjunctions are *and* and *but*
- subordinating, which join a clause of lesser importance to the main clause. Subordinating conjunctions are listed.

Differentiation: Less confident learners should be encouraged to use common sense in choosing suitable conjunctions.

Back at school: Go over the exercise and encourage children to use subordinating conjunctions to create interesting sentences.

Poetry – Unit 2 Classic/narrative poems

Page 120 The Highwayman

Poetry objective: To engage in the active reading of a narrative poem.

Setting the homework: Ensure the poem is read through together and that the children are aware of the power of expression, intonation and action. Possible examples should be given of each.

Differentiation: Less confident learners may wish to focus on one specific area – for example, actions or expression, or just one verse. Different groups could take on different verses.

Back at school: Share some of the performances the children have been practising and possibly record some. Identify the effective elements of each, sharing opinion as to what improves or makes the performance.

Page 121 Creating a scene

Poetry objective: To explore how writers use language to create a dramatic effect.

Setting the homework: Read through the extract and highlight a few key examples. Ensure all children understand what they are looking for in terms of vocabulary and imagery.

Differentiation: Ask children of differing abilities to identify a specific number of examples (maybe four or eight). Ask more confident learners to create their own examples.

Back at school: Discuss and share any examples the children have created themselves.

Page 122 The Mistletoe Bough

Poetry objective: To engage in the active reading of a narrative poem.

Setting the homework: This is a well-written poem with a fascinating story and worthy of extended study. Explain that the best way to bring out the excitement of the story is to read the poem with the rhythm of natural speech, pausing at punctuation, not at the end of lines. Explain to the children that they have to read the poem and retell the story to their helper.

Differentiation: Less confident learners will require help to ensure full understanding of the story in the poem.

Back at school: Talk about the story in the poem and discuss similar incidents today – for example, children who get trapped in abandoned fridges. Further work could include one or more of the following: dramatise the poem; write a prose version or a modern version; study the rhyme and rhythm patterns; study the language.

SCHOLASTIC
www.scholastic.co.uk

Page 123 Meg Merrilies
Poetry objective: To explore how writers use language to create dramatic effects.
Setting the homework: Give the children some brief information about the poet. Despite his short life (1795 to 1821), Keats wrote some of the finest poems in the English language. Page 115 'Poetry analyser' could be used with this poem.
Differentiation: Less confident learners should read the poem with their helper and talk about it. Others should also write about it.
Back at school: The poem is a character description. Read the poem again and discuss what kind of person Meg Merrilies was.

Page 124 All in good clause (3) – Core skills
Objective: To revise the use of clauses in sentence construction.
Setting the homework: Revise necessary terminology – 'noun', 'clause' and 'relative pronoun' (additional relative pronouns are introduced on this page). Go over the explanation and example.
Differentiation: Less confident learners should have no difficulty filling in the gaps by using their common sense to choose suitable relative pronouns from the list.
Back at school: Go over the gap-filling exercise. Review the whole series on clause analysis and encourage the children to use what they have learned to build up interesting sentences in different ways.

Poetry – Unit 3 Choral and performance

Page 125 The Rain-Making Ceremony
Poetry objective: To read performance poetry.
Setting the homework: Explain that this text is from the oral tradition of the Lango people and thus has not been influenced by Western European literary culture. Children should read this aloud with their helper and discuss the importance of rain to the Lango people.
Back at school: Ask for some volunteers to perform the ceremony. Discuss the importance of rain to the Lango people. If time allows, find out more about the Lango people and the climate of Uganda.
Link to *100 Literacy Framework Lessons Y5*: PU3, Phase 1: exploring the features of performance poetry.

Page 126 My Dad, Your Dad
Poetry objective: To read then write performance poetry.
Setting the homework: Explain to the children that the poem is a dialogue poem involving two characters. If they can work with a partner or helper, the activity will be more fun. They will need to use the poem as a model for their own writing. Emphasise that their poems do not have to rhyme and can be based on everyday conversation. They should then be prepared to recite/perform their poem in class.
Back at school: Talk about the poem on the sheet. Divide the class in half, each taking a part and recite the poem. Ask selected children to perform their poems.
Link to *100 Literacy Framework Lessons Y5*: PU3, Phase 1: exploring the features of performance poetry.

Page 127 Onomatopoeia
Poetry objective: To explore features that might make good performance poems.
Setting the homework: Explain the term 'onomatopoeia' by using the explanation.
Differentiation: All children will enjoy playing with the words and writing their own onomatopoeic poems.
Back at school: Share and enjoy the children's onomatopoeic poems.
Link to *100 Literacy Framework Lessons Y5*: PU3, Phase 1: exploring the features of performance poetry; onomatopoeic language.

NARRATIVE

Name   Date

Setting the scene

▪ Read the extract below from *Kensuke's Kingdom* by Michael Morpurgo.

When the beach petered out, we had to strike off into the forest itself. Here too I found a narrow track to follow. The forest became impenetrable at this point, dark and menacing. There was no howling any more, but something infinitely more sinister: the shiver of leaves, the cracking of twigs, sudden surreptitious rustlings, and they were near me, all around me. I knew, I was quite sure now, that eyes were watching us. We were being followed.

▪ In the box provided or on a separate sheet of paper, sketch what you can picture in your imagination when you read the passage above.

▪ As you sketch keep re-reading the passage to ensure you create as detailed a scene as possible.

Text © 1999, Michael Morpurgo.

Dear helper
Objective: To visualise a scene described in a text.
Task: Help your child by reading the extract through together and sharing with them what you see in your imagination. Remind your child that this is not a test of their drawing skills, the task is intended to help them visualise the text.

Name	Date

Beginnings

There are many ways to start a story: with a description of a place or person, with dialogue, writing in the first person (**I**) or an exciting event.

■ Look at the beginnings of these well-known books and decide which one of the beginnings listed above they are using.

■ Explain what it is about each one that makes you want to read on.

'Look out, Willie – the canal…!' Super Gran yelled, as she Super-sprinted across the uneven cobblestones of the towpath towards the boy, her grandson Willard, to save him from a watery grave. (*from* Super Gran Rules OK! *by Forrest Wilson*)

This beginning uses _____

I want to read on because _____

A long time ago, when I was young, on a Wednesday afternoon, a very strange thing happened to me, so strange, you probably won't believe it. That's up to you. Anyway, this is what happened. (*from* Princess by Mistake *by Penelope Lively*)

This beginning uses _____

I want to read on because _____

Deep in the night, thunder crashed in the dark, leaden skies over Transylvania. Brilliant flashes of fork lightening lit up the jagged mountain and the wicked, hideously shaped Castle Duckula, which perched precariously on its summit. (*from* Duckula and the Ghost Train Mystery *by John Broadhead*)

This beginning uses _____

I want to read on because _____

'I'm going shopping in the village,' George's mother said to George on Saturday morning. 'So be a good boy and don't get up to mischief.'

   This was a silly thing to say to a small boy at any time – it immediately made him wonder what sort of mischief he might get up to.
(*from* George's Marvellous Medicine *by Roald Dahl*)

This beginning uses _____

I want to read on because _____

Dear helper
Objective: To compare different story beginnings and talk about what makes a good story beginning.
Task: Read the story beginnings with your child and discuss their characteristics. Ask: *What type is it? What makes you want to read on?* If possible, help your child to find other examples.

NARRATIVE

Name	Date

My favourite author

■ Choose an author that you would like to look at in more detail. Try to gather the information you need to fill in the fact file below.

Author:	
Date of birth:	
Type of books written	
Most famous book:	
Other books written:	
Publisher(s):	
Illustrator(s):	
Key characters:	
Awards:	
Other fascinating facts:	
What other people say about their books:	

Dear helper
Objective: To collect information on a particular author.
Task: Help your child to gather as much information as possible by suggesting suitable internet search engines and/or other sources. Encourage them to do you a one-minute 'Did you know?' style talk about the author when they have finished.

PHOTOCOPIABLE 📖SCHOLASTIC
www.scholastic.co.uk

Name   Date

Phrenological characters

In the 19th century, many people believed that it was possible to read a person's character by the bumps on their head. This so-called 'science' was called **phrenology**. A person who practised the science was called a **phrenologist**.

◼ Imagine you are a phrenologist. Where would you expect to find the bumps on the head of the character you have been reading about? Colour them in on the diagram below.

◼ Write a paragraph describing the character using the words in the areas you shaded. You can use the back of this sheet.

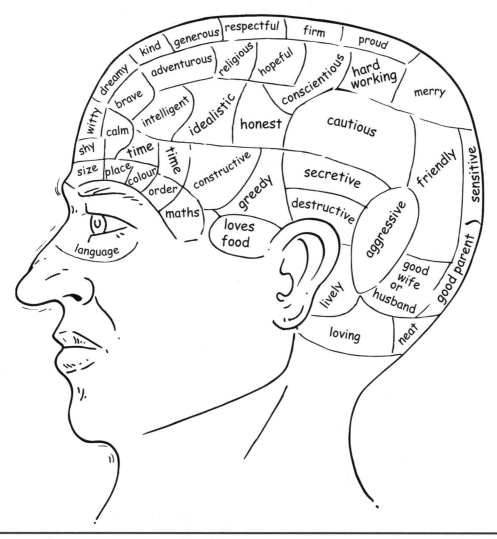

Illustrations © Phil Garner/Beehive Illustration.

Dear helper
Objective: To investigate characters in stories.
Task: Discuss the idea of phrenology with your child. For fun, and as a way of becoming familiar with the diagram, try to read the bumps on each other's heads. Ask your child about the character they have been reading about and discuss which bumps on the diagram should be shaded in.

NARRATIVE

| Name | Date |

Building characters

◼ Read the description below of the character Miss Beckworth from Jacqueline Wilson's *The Lottie Project.*

I *love* mucking about, doing daft things and being a bit cheeky and making everyone laugh. Even the teachers. But the moment I set eyes on Miss Beckworth I knew none of us were going to be laughing. She might be new but she certainly wasn't young. She had grey hair and grey eyes and a grey and white blouse and a grey skirt and laced-up shoes, with a laced-up expression on her face to match. When she spoke her teeth were quite big and stuck out a bit, but I put all thought of Bugs Bunny imitation right out of my head.

There are some teachers – just a few – who have YOU'D BETTER NOT MESS WITH ME! tattooed right across their foreheads. She frowned at me with this incredibly fierce forehead and said, 'Good morning. This isn't a very good start to the new school year.'

I stared at her. What was she on about? Why was she looking at her watch? I wasn't late. OK, the school bell had gone as I was crossing the playground, but you always get five minutes to get to your classroom.

'It's three minutes past nine,' Miss Beckworth announced. 'You're late.'

'No, I'm not,' I said. 'We're not counted late until it's five past.'

I didn't say it cheekily. I was perfectly polite. I was trying to be helpful, actually.

'You're *certainly* not off to a good start,' she goes. 'First you're late. And then you argue. My name's Miss Beckworth. What's your name?'

'Charlie, Miss Beckworth.' (See, *ever* so polite – because I had to pronounce it d-e-l-i-c-a-t-e-l-y.)

'Your proper name?'

'Charlie Enright.'

'We don't seem to be connecting correctly, Miss Enright. Charlie isn't a proper name. It's a diminutive.'

She was trying to make *me* look pretty diminutive, obviously. I was trying to act cool but I could feel my cheeks flushing.

Miss Beckworth

◼ Using different coloured pens, underline or highlight examples of the different ways the author tells us about the character. Think about: description, dialogue and action.

Dear helper

Objective: To identify the different ways characters are developed in writing.

Task: Read the passage and share with your child your thoughts on the character. Encourage them to think about the different ways in which the author presents information about the character.

Name   Date

Character cards

- Think of a name for each of these characters and write it in the box.
- Choose two contrasting characters and write a detailed character sketch for each.

Illustrations © Ray and Corinne Burrows.

Dear helper

Objective: To plan the characters in a story.

Task: Having an idea of how characters might behave and talk, as well as how they look, is an important part of story writing. Support your child by asking questions – for example: *What colour is the character's hair? Is the character kind or cruel? Do they talk in posh or colloquial language?*

NARRATIVE

Name   Date

Tramp trouble

◼ Read this passage which is written from the viewpoint of Bill, who is a tramp.

Bill tried the iron ring on the church door. It turned and the door opened. He sighed with relief. He could sleep snug tonight. Life was getting harder for gentlemen of the road – he didn't like to think of himself as a tramp. Farmers locked their barns, vicars locked their churches – there was no trust these days.

Bill groped his way around the darkened church looking for a good place to sleep. Eventually he settled himself in the choir stalls in the chancel. He took a grubby grey blanket from a plastic bag and spread it over himself. Within minutes he was sound asleep.

Suddenly, he was awoken by the sound of the church door creaking open. 'Oh dear,' he thought. 'What if it is the vicar – still, if it is, perhaps he'll give me a bowl of soup and let me stay here.'

Then he heard the sound of children's voices. Bill hated children because they sometimes teased him or threw things at him. He wondered how he could get rid of them. Should he pretend to be the vicar and order them out, or should he hide and wait for them to go?

'I don't like it,' wailed one voice, 'it's dark and creepy!'

'Course it's creepy!' said another. 'What do you expect on a ghost hunt?'

That gave Bill an idea. He took his old grey blanket and put it round his head so that he looked like the ghost of a monk. Then he started to make a low moaning sound…

◼ Now, rewrite the passage from the viewpoint of the children. You can use the back of this sheet.

◻ Decide how many children there are. Give them names.

◻ What do they do when they hear the moaning?

◻ What do they do when they see 'the ghost of a monk'?

Dear helper

Objective: To retell a story from a different point of view.

Task: Share the reading of the story with your child. Talk about what it must have been like from the children's point of view. This will provide a good foundation for the child's writing.

Name	Date

Time for a break

■ Carefully read the passage below from *The Lottie Project* by Jacqueline Wilson. Think about the different things that are being said and how you could make the writing clearer by dividing it into paragraphs.

■ Using the symbol **//**, mark where the paragraphs should go.

Jo didn't come to bed till very late that night and then she didn't sleep for ages. She tried not to toss and turn but whenever I woke up I knew immediately she was awake. Lying stiff and still, staring up at our crimson ceiling. Only it doesn't look red at night. It's black in the dark. I woke up very early, long before the alarm. At least the ceiling was dimly red now. Jo was properly asleep at last, her hair all sticking up, her mouth slightly open. She had one hand up near her face, clenched in a fist. I propped myself up on one elbow, watching her for a bit, and then I slid out of bed. Jo won't let me stick any posters or magazine pictures up in the living room. We've got a proper print of a plump lady cuddling her daughter with a white frame to match the walls. I didn't want to mess up the round red glow of the bedroom but I've stuck up heaps and heaps of stuff in the loo. Want to see? Of course, it's a bit weird with all those eyes watching you when you go to the toilet. Lisa and Angela always have a giggle about it when they come to my place. They both like my home a lot. They've got much bigger houses but they think mine's best. They're thrilled if I ever have one or other of them to stay over. (They have to come separately – and even then Jo has to sleep on the sofa in the living room.)

Dear helper
Objective: To organise a scene using paragraphs.
Task: Help your child understand paragraphs by talking about the text and how this could be restructured to make it clearer for the reader. Encourage your child to think about where the narrative moves on, as the subject changes.

Editing

- Proofread this story by correcting mistakes in spelling, punctuation and grammar.
- Edit the story by improving the description. There are notes to help you. Use the back of this sheet or a separate piece of paper to rewrite the story.

House of Horror

Chloe and Zoe were trembling with exitement as they went through the turnstile into the theme park.

   'What shall we do first said Chloe'?

   'What about the House of Horror?' said Zoe.

   'Oh look! There's a roller-coaster!' said Chloe.

   'Great! Lets go!' said Zoe.

They qued for twenty minutes until their turn came. The safety bars came down automatically over their shoulders and they were off.

   The ride begins with a slow climb at a steep angle. Then suddenly they sped downwards at great speed. Chloe screamed. Zoe yelled.

   The roller-coaster twisted sharply to the left, went up, then over in a loop-the-loop. Chloe groaned and Zoe was sick.

   Then there was a steep drop. Chloe felt that she had left her stomach behind and Zoe felt dizzy.

   Then the roller-coaster turnd upside down again Chloe's shoe falls off and Zoe lost her purse.

   At last the roller-coaster began to slow down. The girls were wrecked.

   The roller-coaster stopped.

   'That was great!' said Chloe.

   'Yeah,' said Zoe. 'Let's do it again!'

Notes

- spelling
- punctuation
- try some different synonyms of **said** to bring out the girls' excitement.
- punctuation
- spelling
- describe their feelings
- grammar
- Add more description, describing how the girls felt and how they reacted.
- Add to the description of the roller-coaster by adding sounds, sights, and so on.
- spelling
- grammar/punctuation
- Add more description about how wrecked they were.

Dear helper

Objective: To proofread and edit a piece of writing.

Task: This activity will help your child to look critically at a piece of writing to see how it can be improved. This is a skill they should apply to their own writing. The notes will help your child find the mistakes and the sections that need more description. Discuss the suggestions for improving the story.

Name	Date

Which person?

The best way to understand **person** is to look at the verb **to be** written out in full.

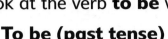

To be (past tense)

Person	Singular	Plural
first	I was	we were
second	you were	you were
third	name/he/she/it was	they were

☐ The **first** and **third person** forms are used to create the 'point of view' in story writing.

☐ The **second person** is used rarely, but may be found in adventure game books and computer games.

◼ Read these story beginnings and say whether they are used in the first, second or third person.

My name is Edward. I am the only survivor of the *SS Albatross* – the only person alive who can tell of the terrible things that happened as she sank below the freezing waves last December.
Person_____

Dougie the dragon was hungry. No tourists had visited his castle for many years. It was time to put an advertisement in the paper.
Person_____

Dear Diary,
This is my second night in the Hotel Transylvania and my host has been very kind to me. Indeed, he has invited me to a feast tomorrow night and he has promised to introduce me to all his friends. He says that I will be the main attraction. I can't wait until tomorrow!

Person_____

You are the officer on duty on the bridge of the *RMS Titanic*. It is night. The sea is calm and perfectly flat. There is no moon and the stars are shining brilliantly. It is chilly – about 32 degrees Farenheit. You are travelling at 21 knots into the darkness. Suddenly you hear a cry from able seaman Fleet in the crow's nest: "Iceberg right ahead!" What will you do?
Person_____

Dear helper
Objective: To identify viewpoint in written texts.
Task: Help your child to relate the explanation of the verb to the texts. If your child needs further support, remind them that *I* or *we* usually indicates that the story is autobiographical or that one of the characters is telling the story in the first person. *He* or *she* indicates the author is telling the story from a third-person perspective. *You* indicates a second-person narrative, where the reader is the one being written about.

Name   Date

Indirect dinosaurs

- Read this playscript with a friend or your helper.
- Underline the **reported speech**.

> **Tip:** look for the phrase
> **N says…**, or **N said that…**
> (N = the name of a person
> or a personal pronoun.)

The scene: *A school corridor. Joe and Flo are coming back to the classroom after delivering the register to the secretary's office.*

Joe: You won't believe what happened to me yesterday.

Flo: Won't I?

Joe: Probably not. I told my sister and she said my imagination was working overtime.

Flo: OK. Try me. My mum says I live in an imaginary world most of the time anyway.

Joe: Well, I was in the library reading this dinosaur book when all of a sudden it started to talk to me.

Flo: What? Have I heard this right? You say that the book you were reading was conversing with you?

Joe: Yes. I mean, not the book exactly, but one of the dinosaurs.

Flo: Oh sure. I think you, my friend, have been watching too many movies.

Joe: I know it sounds crazy, but it's true.

Flo: So, what did Dino have to say to you?

Joe: He said my choice of book was excellent and thanked me for reading it.

Flo: Why would he say that?

Joe: Because he said that as long as people read about dinosaurs, they won't ever really be extinct.

Flo: Not a daft diplo that Dino, eh? So what else did the old fossil have to say?

Just as he says this, Miss Scratchit, the headmistress, comes up.

Miss Scratchit: The old fossil says that the two of you had better get back to your classroom – NOW!

Illustrations © Phil Garner/Beehive Illustration

Dear helper
Objective: Identify direct and indirect (reported) speech.
Task: Take one or more of the parts and read the play with your child. Help them to find and underline the reported speech. Note, there is nothing difficult about direct and reported (or indirect) speech. Remind your child to look for the phrases *says* or *said that*. Reported speech might also be indicated by other verbs that indicate speech, such as *told*, *asked* or *shouted*. There is an example in the script.

Name   Date

Mercury and the Forester

◢ This is a fable (by Aesop). Read it, and then write a few points about how it is different from an ordinary story.

A forester was felling a tree on the bank of a river, when his axe slipped out of his hands and fell into the water. As he stood by the water grumbling about his lost axe, the god Mercury appeared and asked him why he was upset.

When the forester told him, Mercury dived into the river. He came up with a golden axe and asked him if it was the one he had lost. The forester replied that it was not, and Mercury dived a second time. This time he came up with a silver axe.

"No, that is not mine either," said the forester.

Once again Mercury dived into the river, and this time came up with the missing axe. The forester was delighted at having his axe returned, and thanked Mercury warmly. Mercury was so pleased with his honesty that he gave him the other two axes as a reward.

When the forester told the story to his friends, one of them was filled with envy and decided to try his luck in the same way. So he went to fell a tree at the edge of the river, and pretended to drop his axe into the water. Mercury appeared as before and offered to find the lost axe. He dived in and came up with a golden axe just as he had done before. Without waiting to be asked whether it was his or not, the man cried, "That's mine, that's mine!" and tried to grab the precious object. But Mercury was so disgusted at his dishonesty that he refused to give him the golden axe, and also refused to find the one he had lost.

Moral: Honesty is the best policy.

Notes on differences:

Extension

◢ Write your own fable which ends with the same moral. Use the back of this sheet.

Dear helper
Objective: To identify the features of fables.
Task: Share the reading of this fable with your child. Then, discuss how it is different from an ordinary story. Ask: *What is the last line of the story?*

NARRATIVE

Name   Date

The Mouse and the Lion

◼ Read this fable from Aesop.

One day a tiny mouse came upon a sleeping lion. The cheeky mouse decided to have some fun and ran all over the lion's head. Before long, the lion woke up and opened his huge jaws to swallow the mouse.

"Oh please, sir, forgive me and do not eat me," cried the mouse. "I may be able to help you one day!"

The idea that such a tiny creature would be able to help him amused the lion so much that he let the mouse go. But a few days later, the lion was caught in a snare. He couldn't set himself free but the mouse heard his roars and ran to help. The mouse quickly gnawed through the ropes and the lion was free once more.

Moral: Little friends may prove great friends.

◼ What are the main themes or features that you will also find in other Aesop's fables? Jot down your ideas below.

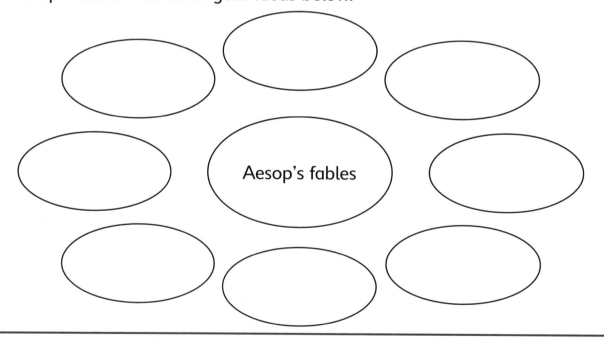

Aesop's fables

Dear helper
Objective: To identify the features of Aesop's fables.
Task: Your child will have read other examples of Aesop's fables in school. Read the fable through and ask them to identify recurring themes and features. Many versions of Aesop's fables are available online if you and your child would like to read more examples.

PHOTOCOPIABLE ◼SCHOLASTIC

www.scholastic.co.uk

Name   Date

Character thoughts

■ Read this extract from a version of Robin Hood and think about what Robin might be feeling or thinking.

Now he was face to face with the Sheriff himself. Their swords crossed. Robin's sped upwards, throwing the Sheriff's blade aside. Then he brought his own down two-handed on his adversary's head.

With a grinding clash, the sword broke on the Sheriff's helmet.

"Curse the smith that made you," he swore.

"Take him alive," yelled the Sheriff.

The struggle lasted only a brief moment, then Robin Hood was overpowered and dragged away.

from The Story of Robin Hood *retold by Robert Leeson*

■ Complete the thought bubbles around the character's head with your main ideas. If you run out of room use another sheet of paper.

Dear helper
Objective: To consider what a character might be thinking.
Task: Read the passage with your child and discuss what the character might be thinking. Encourage your child to jot down notes as you talk, then to decide what to include in the thought bubbles.

NARRATIVE

Name   Date

The Diary of Robin Hood

■ Read this extract from a version of Robin Hood and think about what Robin might be feeling or thinking. If Robin went home and wrote in his diary straight after this what do you think he would say? Write your diary entry on a separate sheet of paper.

The wooden bridge was only wide enough for one and there was a man on the planks already, so big he blocked the bridge from rail to rail. Robin stepped on lightly to see if the stranger would make room for him.

Instead he spoke roughly: "You stand back till I cross, lad, or I'll give you a taste of this on your back." And he wagged a great quarterstaff at Robin, who did not take that kindly at all.

Quick as light Robin unslung his bow, slipped an arrow from the quiver at his side and notched it.

"Don't talk like a fool, man," he called. "I could send this through your heart before you could even touch me."

The stranger eyed the arrow point aimed at his chest and answered scornfully: "Spoken like a true coward. Bow against staff? What match is that?"

Robin flushed red with anger. "Coward? Not me. If that's what you think, I'll put my bow down and fight you hand to hand."

Then he got back his good humour and, whistling, ran to the bushes to cut himself an oak staff with his hunting knife. Trimming twigs and leaves, he hastened back to the bridge.

"Right, friend," he said cheerfully. "Let's give it a trial. The one who puts the other in the water is free to cross."

"Agreed!" With that the other swung his stick across his chest as Robin rushed forward, oak branch whirling. He came on so fast the big man was taken aback and took a knock on the crown that flayed his skin and sent the blood streaming down.

"One to you," he grunted. "But I pay my debts." He switched hands so rapidly that Robin never saw the blow until it caught him across the back and drove the breath from his chest.

Then it was thrust, strike and block like farmers threshing corn, till all of a sudden Robin felt the end of the stranger's staff deep in his belly, followed by one across his head that tipped him like a sack of corn over the rail and into the swiftly-flowing brook.

As Robin struggled in the water, the giant, wiping the sweat from his red face, leaned over the rail. When he got back his breath he shouted, "Now where are you, me lad?"

Robin spluttered and laughed and yelled back, "Going downstream fast."

from The Story of Robin Hood *retold by Robert Leeson*

Text extract © 1996 Robert Leeson; illustrations © Phil Garner/Beehive Illustration

Dear helper
Objective: To consider what a character is thinking.
Task: Read the extract through with your child and discuss what the character's thoughts might be. Listen to your child's diary entry when they have completed it.

Name   Date

A tale to tell

◼ Think of the classic story of Robin Hood. Think about how you could retell this to younger children. Use the notes below to help you and add any additional notes in the spaces.

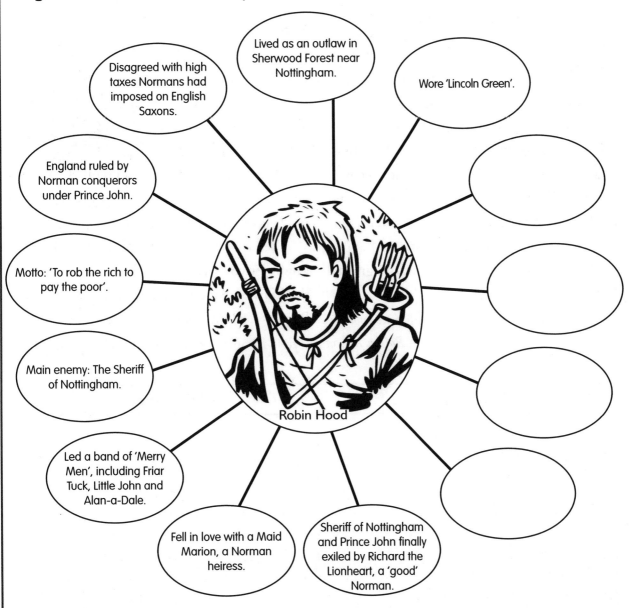

Lived as an outlaw in Sherwood Forest near Nottingham.

Disagreed with high taxes Normans had imposed on English Saxons.

Wore 'Lincoln Green'.

England ruled by Norman conquerors under Prince John.

Motto: 'To rob the rich to pay the poor'.

Main enemy: The Sheriff of Nottingham.

Led a band of 'Merry Men', including Friar Tuck, Little John and Alan-a-Dale.

Robin Hood

Fell in love with a Maid Marion, a Norman heiress.

Sheriff of Nottingham and Prince John finally exiled by Richard the Lionheart, a 'good' Norman.

◼ Make sure you think about vocabulary and what the important parts of the story are. What will younger children particularly like? Is it the right length?

Dear helper
Objective: To retell a story for young children.
Task: Help your child to use the notes to create a story that they can tell orally. It may help to cut out and arrange the notes, adding children's own ideas. Talk about appropriate language for a younger audience and if possible look at some stories written for younger children.

NARRATIVE

Name   Date

The same but different

● Read the passages below from different versions of Robin Hood. Think about how they are similar and how they are different and jot down your ideas in the table.

Extract 1

Here was a friar right enough. His corpulent body with its curving belly was clad in a brown robe, tucked up at the knee to show brawny bare legs and huge feet in sandals. Around his head was a fringe of thick brown hair. But sitting on top of the tonsure was a helmet as bright as Robin's. And around his waist was no cord but a leather belt, with sword and dagger. A buckler likewise covered his left!

"Pax vobiscum, my son," the friar greeted him. "Peace be with you."

from The Story of Robin Hood *retold by Robert Leeson*

Extract 2

"I'm looking for Robin Hood. Do you know the rogue?" Robin saw the man was wearing the brown habit of a friar.

"I've heard of him," Robin replied. 'Now will you let me up?" But the friar put his foot on Robin's chest and would not let him move.

"Tell me where I can find him and I might let you live, by God's good grace," said the friar, pressing the point of his sword into Robin's neck just enough to draw blood.

from Robin Of Sherwood *by Michael Morpurgo*

Similarities	**Differences**

Text extracts © 1996, Robert Leeson and © 1996, Michael Morpurgo; illustrations © Phil Garner/Beehive Illustration

Dear helper
Objective: To read and understand the differences between different versions of the same story.
Task: Help your child to see the differences between the two versions and talk about why this might be – a different audience, a modern version, different style and so on.

PHOTOCOPIABLE ■■SCHOLASTIC
www.scholastic.co.uk

NARRATIVE

Name	Date

Arthur: chosen king

◼ Read this famous passage from the legend of King Arthur.

◼ Write your version of the episode. You can use the back of the sheet or a separate piece of paper.

Illustrations © Phil Garner/Beehive Illustration.

On Christmas Eve, Bishop Brice spoke to the nobles of Britain in the great church at Winchester. When the service ended, a miraculous stone was found outside the church. In the stone was firmly fixed a sword, with the following words engraved on its hilt:

> 'I am the sword Excalibur,
> A sword only a king can draw.'

Bishop Brice gave thanks to God and ordered that whoever could draw out the sword from the stone should be acknowledged as the rightful king of the Britons. The most famous knights, one after another, tried their strength, but the miraculous sword would not be moved. It stayed there until Candlemas, until Easter, and until Pentecost, when the best knights in the kingdom assembled for the annual tournament.

Arthur, who was at that time serving as a squire to Sir Kay, came with him to the tournament that year. Sir Kay fought with great success in the tournament, but unluckily broke his sword in one of the bouts. He sent Arthur for a new one. Arthur hurried home, but saw the sword in the stone, and decided to save himself a long journey. He drew the sword out quite easily and took it to his master.

When Sir Kay saw the sword, he recognised it by the engraving on its hilt and asked Arthur how he got it. 'I just pulled it out,' said Arthur. Sir Kay, still doubting, took Arthur to the stone, and thrust the sword back in to see if he could pull it out again. By this time, a large crowd had gathered. First, Sir Kay tried to pull it out himself, but though he heaved with all his might, it would not give an inch. Then he asked Arthur to try. Arthur stepped up to the stone and pulled out the sword as smoothly as from a well-greased scabbard.

Sir Kay, and all present, kneeled before him and proclaimed him king.

Dear helper
Objective: To write a version of a known legend.
Task: Share the reading of this passage with your child. Then, talk about the many different ways in which the story has been retold. Help your child to decide on a way of retelling the story.

NARRATIVE

Name   Date

The Lambton Worm

● Read this 'choice' story. Experiment with different choices.

1. Long ago, in the Middle Ages, at a place called Lambton, a young man caught a strange worm when he was fishing. The worm was like nothing he had ever seen before. It had scales, four tiny legs, and a mouthful of sharp teeth.

If you think he should throw it back, go to 2. If you think he should kill it, go to 3.

_____

2. Over the next few years, the worm grew to an enormous size and started to feed on sheep, and cattle, and sometimes even the people of Lambton. The young man realised that it was the same worm that he had let go, and wondered if he should do something to help.

If you think he should try to kill it, go to 3. If you think he should keep quiet, go to 4.

_____

3. He tried to kill the worm by cutting it in half, but the two halves wriggled back together and joined up again no matter how many times he tried. This worried him very much because the worm was growing quickly.

If you think he should give up, go to 4. If you think he should seek the help of the wise woman, go to 5.

_____

4. The worm grew even bigger and stronger. It ate all the sheep and cattle and killed so many people, that those who were left decided to go away. That is why all that is left of the town of Lambton today, is a desolate heath and a few scattered ruins. THE END

_____

5. The wise woman said: "The only way to kill the worm, now that it is so big, is to cover your armour with many sharp blades and fight the worm in the middle of the river."

If you think that is bad advice, go to 4. If you think it is worth a try, go to 6.

_____

6. The young man followed the wise woman's instructions and waited for the worm in the river. The worm attacked by wrapping itself around him, trying to crush him to death — but the blades cut the worm into many parts and the river swept the parts away before they could join up again. The worm was dead and the people of Lambton were safe at last. THE END

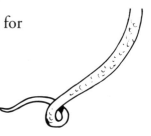

Illustrations © Phil Garner/Beehive Illustration

Dear helper
Objective: To write a version of a legend.
Task: Read each section with your child. Discuss and experiment with the choices given. Which choices did your child think made for the best story? Encourage and help your child to retell another legend as a 'choice' story.

Name	Date

Full to -ful

The suffix **-ful** added to a noun, turns the noun into an adjective which usually means 'full of'. For example:

beauty → beautiful = 'full of beauty'

Rules:

☐ **-ful** as a suffix has only one **l** – for example, **hopeful**.

☐ **y** changes to **i** when a suffix is added – for example, **pitiful**.

◼ Complete the **adjective** column by adding **-ful** to the nouns and changing **y** to **i** if necessary.

Noun	Adjective
beauty	beautiful
care	
cheer	
deceit	
disgrace	
duty	
fancy	
grace	
hope	
mercy	
peace	
pity	
plenty	
spite	
success	

Some words ending in **-ful** can be made to mean the opposite by changing **-ful** for **-less** – for example, **careless**.

◼ Write down words from the above list that can be made to mean the opposite. Use the back of this sheet.

Dear helper

Objective: To explore spelling patterns: adding the suffix '-ful'.

Task: Remind your child that a suffix is a group of letters added to the end of a word to change its meaning or use. Check that your child takes care to apply the two rules, especially with the words ending in '-y'.

What do you do?

The suffix **-cian** means: someone who works with that subject.

Usually, the suffix **-cian** is added without any change to the root word. In some cases the word may already have a suffix that has to be removed. Just use common sense, as all the words are well known.

◼ Look at these pictures of people doing their jobs. Write the appropriate **-cian** word underneath.

politics	diet	beauty

music	optics	physics
	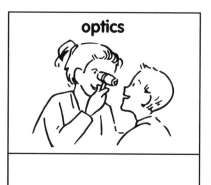	

electric	magic	mathematics

Illustrations © Phil Garner/Beehive Illustration

Dear helper

Objective: To recognise and spell the suffix '-cian'.

Task: Remind your child that a root is the basic part of a word to which letters (a suffix) can be added at the end to change its meaning or use. Your child may need help when adapting the root word to fit the suffix so that the resulting word is spelled correctly.

Name			Date

Opposites by prefix

■ Add the correct **prefix** to make the words below mean the opposite. The first one has been done as an example. Note that the spelling of the root word does not change when the prefix is added.

■ Select from the following prefixes:

ab- dis- il- im- in- ir- mis- un-

dis	advantage		like
	approve		lock
	audible		moral
	aware		mortal
	behave		necessary
	comfortable		normal
	connect		obey
	convenient		order
	correct		perfect
	essential		pleasure
	fair		polite
	happy		possible
	human		regular
	kind		sane
	legal		visible
	legible		wise

Dear helper

Objective: To investigate opposites.

Task: Remind your child that a prefix is a group of letters added to the beginning of a word to change its meaning. Read each word to your child. Check that they understand it, then ask: *What is its opposite?* The list of prefixes can then be used as prompts and aids to spelling.

Name   Date

Stories from around the world

■ Can you think of or find books, TV programmes or stories that are based in different parts of the world? Try to find at least one for each of the sections below, then state how you knew it was from that area.

	Story, film, TV programme	How you knew
Africa		
Australia		
Europe		
Caribbean		
India		
Other:		

Dear helper
Objective: To see how we can gain information about other cultures through literature, TV and film.
Task: First of all, ask your child if they know of any stories, films or TV programmes from each of the places listed. Then encourage them to carry out research to fill in the gaps.

Name	Date

Spot the difference

■ Carefully read the passages below and highlight anything that tells you the stories are set in a different culture from our own.

The children of Pleasance, by the coast, came out to play. There were roasting crabs, sweet potatoes and plantains on an open fire. The local old man came to sit, as he usually did, to eat with the children. The old man, whose name no one knew, held a plantain in his hand, and the children knew at once that there would be a story, and that it would contain plantains. The old man always told them stories about things he held in his hand or was pointing to.   *From* Bre-nancy and the 13 Plantains *by Petronella Breinburg*

Toewi liked to imagine things. She often pretended to herself that she had flown away into the sky to be a young princess, married to the sky prince. Then, she would sing and dance around. Toewi also had to do chores; she had to fetch water from the river, and to help with the weaving of cotton into cloth, but she didn't mind the chores. She sang happily while carrying water on her shoulder or while weaving.   *From* Toewi and Kroemoe *by Petronella Breinburg*

■ Where do you think the stories might be set? How could you find out?

_____

_____

_____

Text extracts © 1999, Petronella Breinburg.

Dear helper
Objective: To identify cultural differences shown in a text.
Task: Read the passages through with your child and talk about words and phrases that tell us that the stories are from a different culture. Some will be more obvious than others.

NARRATIVE

Name   Date

Culture clues

◼ Write a passage about your day which reflects the way we live in Britain in the 21st century. It could contain references to food, clothes, music, technology, other people, events, home life, family, leisure, work and so on. Try to make it as representative of our country today as you can!

◼ Imagine if someone somewhere else in the world were to read it. What would it tell them about living in Britain today?

Illustrations © Phil Garner/Beehive Illustration.

Dear helper
Objective: To see how language can show cultural differences.
Task: Ask your child to consider what makes our culture what it is. Discuss what your child has done today that is typical of our culture. When your child has finished, read through their work and talk about the things they have included.

Name	Date

A different point of view

■ Read the extract carefully and decide what Bre-nancy and Ma-nancy may be thinking or feeling. Record your ideas in the thought bubbles.

'"Come on, my friend…" Bre-nancy gave Bre-bush Rat a very friendly smile. "I'll help carry it and you give me some for my family, eh? I don't want any for myself, only for the wife and children, I swear."

'"OK, then." Bre-bush Rat gave Bre-nancy exactly thirteen plantains, one for each of his children and one for his wife.

'Bre-nancy got home and watched his wife roast the plantains and give one to each of his children and keep one for herself. He sat down and made his face look as sad as possible.

'"Oh," said Ma-nancy, "you take mine." And she pushed her plantain in front of Bre-nancy. "No, no." he said.

'"You have half of mine," said the first child and at once broke the plantain in half.

'"And half of mine," said the second, then the third and then the fourth. Soon each child had given half of their plantain to their dad. Each time Bre-nancy at first refused but then took it and ate it all up.

'Ma-nancy had an idea,' remembered the old man.

'"Tell me good husband how many half plantain have you ate and how many whole plantains that makes?"

'"Oh, eh, eh,.." Poor Bre-nancy. He could not say. He got out and began to walk up and down with two of his legs behind his back. And he still is walking now, trying to do his sums.'

From Bre-nancy and the 13 Plantains *by Petronella Breinburg*

Dear helper
Objective: To explore a story from different characters' viewpoints.
Task: Encourage your child to study the text and tell you about each character. You could ask them questions about what they tell you and to give reasons for their views.

Name	Date

A letter to...

◼ Read the passage below from a story called *Papa Bois* by Petronella Breinburg.

Tara was unhappy and sulking; she did not want to take her cousin Lennet and parents up and down Mount Aripo to see the scenery. Tara wanted to be with her friends in San Fernando. She and her friends were selected to help build the Tadjan for the Hosay parade.

Besides, Tara couldn't stand her cousin's bragging any longer. According to her, everything in Surinam was better than Trinidad and Tobago. The Hosay Tadjan in Surinam was apparently the best in the world; far better than the one in Trinidad. Even the picnic that Tara's mother prepared was not as good as that of Surinam.

'In Surinam,' said the cousin, 'roti does not have peas in it. The thing with peas in it is dall pori not roti.' Tara turned to look through the window while her cousin continued: 'In Surinam, our cars don't break down, we don't get stuck on mountains in broken cars. In Surinam…'

◼ Imagine you are Tara writing to your friends about your cousin Lennet and write your letter below. Think carefully about how she might write.

Dear friends
From Tara

Text extract © 1999, Petronella Breinburg.

Dear helper
Objective: To write as a particular character.
Task: Help your child to understand the format and style of a letter. To help them structure the letter, encourage them to tell you about the character they are writing as.

Name	Date

Caribbean folk tale

Spoken language features:

- ☐ incomplete sentences
- ☐ importance of tone of voice
- ☐ use of gesture, facial expression
- ☐ simple plot structure
- ☐ informal style, perhaps with dialect.

Written language features:

- ☐ carefully constructed sentences
- ☐ punctuation to help the reader
- ☐ more detail in descriptions
- ☐ more complex plot structure
- ☐ more formal style.

◼ Find and underline examples of the features of **spoken** language in this oral version of a Caribbean folk tale.

Let me tell 'ee the story of Rose Hall – that was one big house! – the best in Jamaica, folks say. Well, it was owned by John Palmer – he be one of them colonial planters – worth a fortune a was and all from the hard work of black brothers and sisters. (*Sadly.*) Slaves, they was. Well. His troubles began when he brought a bride back to Rose Hall – that was 1820, I mind. At first they was happy enough, but Annie, well a was only 18, and she soon got tired o' that lardy husband – well, he was old man, do yo see, and she was young girl – so she takes up wi' a young man – a slave, he was. When her husband find out, he go stark staring mad and they had real bad argument. (*Frowns.*) Soon after, John Palmer, he was found dead. Well, they blame Annie. They say that she got her lover to strangle him. Soon after that she had the slave whip to death so as to get rid of the only witness. Well, Annie was master now – and a cruel one! (*Gestures as if using a rod.*) She rule the estate with a rod of iron – ooh and was she bad to her slaves! One day she whip a slave so bad that his back was ripped open 'til yo could see the bone! (*Shakes head.*) That boy was so wild wi' pain he broke loose and tried to strangle her. Ha, ha – the best part is that when she cry for help, the other slaves, they help him – not her! They put a mattress on her and jump on it until she was suffocated to death – serve her right too! (*Grins and nods.*) They say she haunt the place now. (*Frowns.*). Well, guess what – that old place – Rose Hall – was a ruin for years, but now they've done it all up – the Jamaican government – for tourists – ha ha – but yo wouldn't catch me goin' there (*waves hand*) – no, no, not with the ghost of old Annie and all!

Extension

◼ Change the oral story into a written story. Use a separate sheet of paper.

Dear helper

Objective: To be aware of the differences between spoken and written language.

Task: This activity should help your child understand how meaning is conveyed in spoken language through context, tone of voice, facial expression and gesture. In written language, all this has to be conveyed through word choice, sentence construction and punctuation. Read the story to your child, trying to make it as authentically 'oral' as possible. Alternatively, tell your child an oral story of your own and then ask: *How would it be different if it were written in a book?*

Name   Date

Don't take it literally

■ Study this table which explains the terms **literal**, **figurative**, **metaphor** and **simile**.

■ Add your own examples to the table. Some have been started for you.

Literal: Straightforward, factual way of saying something.	Figurative: An imaginative way of saying something, often by comparing one thing to another.	
	Simile A comparison using like or as.	**Metaphor** A direct comparison, saying one thing is another.
My feet are cold.	My feet are like ice.	My feet are ice.
Ordinary post is slow.	Ordinary post is as slow as a snail.	Original post is snail mail.
He is tall.	He is as tall as a giant.	He is a giant of a man.

Dear helper

Objective: To investigate language that creates images in the reader's mind.

Task: Understanding how language can be used to heighten description will help your child appreciate it in reading and, hopefully, apply it to their writing. Take the time to go over the explanation in the table, adding your own examples.

Name	Date

Linstead Market

Accent means variation in pronunciation.
Dialect means variation in vocabulary and grammar.

- Read the poem.
- Underline differences of **accent**.
- Highlight differences in **dialect**.
- Work out from the context what the dialect words mean.

Linstead Market

Carry me ackee go a Linstead market:
Not a quatty wut sell.
Carry me ackee go a Linstead market:
Not a quatty wut sell.
Chorus   Lard, wat a night, not a bite,
              Wat a Satiday night.
              Lard, wat night, not a bite,
              Wat a Satiday night.

Everybody come feel up, feel up:
Not a quatty wut sell.
Everybody come feel up, squeeze up:
Not a quatty wut sell.
Chorus

Mek me call i' louder: ackee! ackee!
Red an pretty dem 'tan!
Lady, buy yu Sunday marnin brukfas',
Rice an ackee nyam gran'.
Chorus

All de pickney dem a linga, linga,
Fe weh dem mumma no bring.
All de pickney dem a linga, linga,
Fe weh dem mumma no bring.
Chorus
Traditional Caribbean

Illustrations © Phil Garner/Beehive Illustration.

Dear helper
Objective: To understand how words vary across dialects.
Task: Enjoy reading this poem aloud with your child (for example, by sharing verses). Help your child to guess from the context what the dialect words might mean. They will be explained by the teacher back in the classroom.

Name   Date

The Secret Garden

This is the opening to the famous novel, The Secret Garden, *written in 1911.*

- Read the extract aloud. Note the punctuation – the sentences are very long!
- Underline all the words and phrases that describe Mary.

When Mary Lennox was sent to Misselthwaite Manor to live with her uncle, everybody said she was the most disagreeable-looking child ever seen. It was true, too. She had a little thin face and a little thin body, thin light hair and a sour expression. Her hair was yellow, and her face was yellow because she had been born in India and had always been ill in one way or another. Her father had held a position under the English Government and had always been busy and ill himself, and her mother had been a great beauty who cared only to go to parties and amuse herself with carefree people. She had not wanted a little girl at all, and when Mary was born she handed her over to the care of an Ayah*, who was made to understand that if she wished to please the Memsahib** she must keep the child out of sight as much as possible. So, when she was a sickly, fretful, ugly little baby she was kept out of the way, and when she became a sickly, fretful, toddling thing she was kept out of the way also. She never remembered seeing familiarly anything but the dark faces of her Ayah and the other native servants, and as they always obeyed her and gave her her own way in everything, because the Memsahib would be angry if she was disturbed by her crying, by the time she was six years old she was as tyrannical and selfish a little pig as ever lived.

Frances Hodgson Burnett

*Ayah = servant; nanny **Memsahib = mistress of the house*

Extension

- The last sentence is made up of many clauses. Rewrite the sentence as three separate sentences. Use the back of this sheet.

Illustrations © Phil Garner/Beehive Illustration.

Dear helper
Objective: To explore older literature, such as extracts from classic serials.
Task: Read this extract with your child. The vocabulary is not difficult, but the sentence construction is challenging. Encourage your child to notice the punctuation. Discuss the description of Mary. Ask: *Does it give a good mental picture of what the girl was like?* If your child does the extension activity, help them to find the three sentences in one.

PHOTOCOPIABLE **SCHOLASTIC**
www.scholastic.co.uk

Name	Date

Shakespeare's language

Julius Caesar was written in 1597 by William Shakespeare. It tells the story of the first Roman emperor, who was assassinated by Brutus. In this scene, Caesar's wife, Calpurnia, tries to stop Caesar going out to the Senate because she has seen and heard about some frightening signs.

◼ Read this scene aloud.

◼ Rewrite the scene in simple modern English using the glossary to help you. Use a separate sheet.

	Glossary
Calpurnia:	
Caesar, I never *stood on ceremonies,*	believed in signs
Yet now they *fright* me. There is *one within,*	frighten, someone inside
Besides the things that we have heard and seen,	
Recounts most *horrid* sights seen by the *watch.*	tells of/horrible/guards
A lioness hath *whelped* in the streets;	given birth
And graves have yawned, and *yielded* up their dead;	given
Fierce fiery warriors fought upon the clouds,	
In ranks and squadrons *and right form of* war,	just like a real
Which drizzled blood upon the Capitol;	
The noise of battle hurtled in the air,	
Horses *did neigh,* and dying men *did groan,*	neighed/groaned
And ghosts *did shriek* and squeal about the streets.	shrieked
O Caesar! These things are *beyond all use,*	not normal
And I do fear them.	
Caesar:	
What can be avoided	
Whose end is *purposed* by the mighty gods?	intended
Yet Caesar shall go *forth;* for these predictions	out
Are *to the world in general* as to Caesar.	for everybody
Calpurnia:	
When beggars die, there are no comets seen;	
The heavens themselves blaze forth the death of princes.	
Caesar:	
Cowards die many times before their deaths;	
The *valiant* never taste of death but once.	brave

Illustrations © Phil Garner/Beehive Illustration.

Dear helper
Objective: To explore the challenge and appeal of older literature.
Task: Read this scene a number of times with your child, taking different parts each time. On one of the readings, substitute the words in the glossary for those in italics.

NARRATIVE

Name   Date

Treasure Island

◼ Read the extract below from *Treasure Island* by Robert Louis Stevenson (1883). What evidence can you find in the text that tells us that the story was written many years ago? Highlight words and phrases in the text.

When I returned with the rum, they were already seated on either side of the captain's breakfast-table—Black Dog next to the door and sitting sideways so as to have one eye on his old shipmate and one, as I thought, on his retreat.

He bade me go and leave the door wide open. "None of your keyholes for me, sonny," he said; and I left them together and retired into the bar.

"For a long time, though I certainly did my best to listen, I could hear nothing but a low gattling; but at last the voices began to grow higher, and I could pick up a word or two, mostly oaths, from the captain.

"No, no, no, no; and an end of it!" he cried once. And again, "If it comes to swinging, swing all, say I."

Then all of a sudden there was a tremendous explosion of oaths and other noises—the chair and table went over in a lump, a clash of steel followed, and then a cry of pain, and the next instant I saw Black Dog in full flight, and the captain hotly pursuing, both with drawn cutlasses, and the former streaming blood from the left shoulder. Just at the door the captain aimed at the fugitive one last tremendous cut, which would certainly have split him to the chine had it not been intercepted by our big signboard of Admiral Benbow. You may see the notch on the lower side of the frame to this day.

◼ Do you know or can you find any other stories that were written at this time by the same or different authors?

Illustrations © Phil Garner/Beehive Illustration.

Dear helper
Objective: To experience some older literature.
Task: Explore the passage with your child and encourage them to look for clues in the text that tell us it is from older literature. If you can, share some other older texts with them, such as *Black Beauty, Little Women, Oliver Twist* and *The Children of The New Forest.*

Name   Date

Illustrations © Phil Garner/Beehive Illustration.

The Jungle Book

■ Think about the story of *The Jungle Book* by Rudyard Kipling. A passage is included below. Can you rewrite this for a modern audience? Think about vocabulary that may need to be updated and the style of writing.

"Listen, man-cub," said the Bear, and his voice rumbled like thunder on a hot night. "I have taught thee all the Law of the Jungle for all the peoples of the jungle—except the Monkey-Folk who live in the trees. They have no law. They are outcasts. They have no speech of their own, but use the stolen words which they overhear when they listen, and peep, and wait up above in the branches. Their way is not our way. They are without leaders. They have no remembrance. They boast and chatter and pretend that they are a great people about to do great affairs in the jungle, but the falling of a nut turns their minds to laughter and all is forgotten. We of the jungle have no dealings with them. We do not drink where the monkeys drink; we do not go where the monkeys go; we do not hunt where they hunt; we do not die where they die. Hast thou ever heard me speak of the Bandar-log till today?"

Dear helper
Objective: To rewrite older literature for a modern audience.
Task: Share the older story with your child and then talk about the parts that could be changed or might need to be changed to cater for a modern audience.

NARRATIVE

Name   Date

Desert island

◀ Read this extract from the beginning of *Robinson Crusoe* by Daniel Defoe (published in 1719).

◀ Write a continuation describing how the ship sinks and Robinson Crusoe manages to get to an island and survive. Do not try to follow the original story – use your own ideas. Write in the same style, using the first person (**I**) and make the language sound old fashioned. Use a separate sheet.

By this time it blew a terrible storm indeed, and now I began to see terror and amazement in the faces even of the seamen themselves. The master, though vigilant in the business of preserving the ship, yet as he went in and out of his cabin by me, I could hear him softly to himself say several times, 'Lord, be merciful to us, we shall be all lost, we shall be all undone'; and the like.

During these first hurries, I was stupid, lying still in my cabin, which was in the steerage, and cannot describe my temper. I could ill reassume the first penitence which I had so apparently trampled upon, and hardened myself against. I thought the bitterness of death had been past, and that this would be nothing too, like the first. But when the master himself came by me, as I said just now, and said we should be all lost, I was dreadfully frighted. I got up out of my cabin and looked out; but such a dismal sight I never saw. The sea went mountains high, and broke upon us every three or four minutes.

When I could look about, I could see nothing but distress round us: Two ships that rid near us, we found, had cut their masts by the board, being deep loaden; and our men cried out that a ship which rid about a mile ahead of us was foundered. Two more ships, being driven from their anchors, were run out of the roads to sea at all adventures, and that with not a mast standing.

Illustrations © Phil Garner/Beehive Illustration.

Dear helper
Objective: To write in the style of a given author.
Task: Read this extract with your child. Don't worry about understanding all the archaic language. It is the gist of the story and a general feeling for the old-fashioned style that is important for the activity. Discuss what might happen on the island – make up new adventures. Talk about how to write the continuation using Defoe's style.

PHOTOCOPIABLE 🔲 SCHOLASTIC
www.scholastic.co.uk

Name   Date

In the style of...

◼ Below is an excerpt from *Treasure Island* by Robert Louis Stevenson (1883). Read the text and think about how the author writes.

I was surprised at the coolness with which John avowed his knowledge of the island, and I own I was half-frightened when I saw him drawing nearer to myself. He did not know, to be sure, that I had overheard his council from the apple barrel, and yet I had by this time taken such a horror of his cruelty, duplicity, and power that I could scarce conceal a shudder when he laid his hand upon my arm.

"Ah," says he, "this here is a sweet spot, this island—a sweet spot for a lad to get ashore on. You'll bathe, and you'll climb trees, and you'll hunt goats, you will; and you'll get aloft on them hills like a goat yourself. Why, it makes me young again. I was going to forget my timber leg, I was. It's a pleasant thing to be young and have ten toes, and you may lay to that. When you want to go a bit of exploring, you just ask old John, and he'll put up a snack for you to take along."

And clapping me in the friendliest way upon the shoulder, he hobbled off forward and went below.

◼ Try to write the next paragraph or two of the story in Robert Louis Stevenson's style of writing. Think about:
   ☐ Where did the narrator go next?
   ☐ Did he follow Long John Silver?
   ☐ Did they speak to each other again?
   ☐ Where did they go?

Dear helper
Objective: To write in the style of a specific author.
Task: Talk about the author and his writing and encourage the children try out some sentences orally first to see if they fit in with the author's style.

Direct and reported

Direct speech uses words actually spoken using speech marks.

Reported (or indirect) speech states what was said rather than using the actual words spoken. Speech marks are not used.

Rules for changing direct to reported speech:

☐ Speech marks are not used.

☐ Reporting clause is replaced by an introductory clause often ending with **that**. Often, the tense changes from present to past.

☐ Personal pronouns change: first- and second-person pronouns become third-person pronouns.

◼ Change these examples of **direct speech** into **indirect speech**.

"My face feels all itchy," said Sarah.

_____

"I'm only joking," laughed Dad.

_____

"I don't want to stay out past midnight," said Simon.

_____

"I'm not afraid of spiders," said Sunil.

_____

◼ Change these examples of **indirect speech** into **direct speech**.

Tim said that he really hated going to the dentist.

_____

Zoe said that she was going to stay in to wash her hair.

_____

Joe shouted to the taxi driver to hurry up.

_____

Shona asked her mum if she could have a party.

_____

Dear helper

Objective: Changing between direct and reported speech.

Task: Help your child to apply the rules to the sentences. A good way to do this is to ask questions like: *What did Sarah say?* for the first set of questions, and: *What were Tim's actual words?* for the second set.

Name	Date

Old new school

Dialogue is set out with a new indented line for each change of speaker.

☐ It is punctuated with speech marks.

☐ A capital letter is used after the first speech mark.

☐ A comma, question mark or exclamation mark is used before the final speech mark.

◀ Use different coloured pens to highlight:

   ☐ the new indented lines that show the changes of speaker

   ☐ the speech marks

   ☐ the other punctuation marks.

The building was at least a hundred years old. The windows were arched, like a church's, and the woodwork was full of wormholes. It looked more like a set for a horror film than a school.

'I'm not going in!' said Simon.

'But you have to,' said his mum, patiently. 'It's the law. Every child has to go to school.'

'But it looks haunted!' wailed Simon.

'Nonsense!' snapped his mum. 'You've been watching too many horror films.'

She took Simon to the door and watched him go in. He crept down the gloomy corridor, wondering where to go, when a harsh voice snapped, 'You, boy, get into the classroom at once!'

Simon turned round and to his horror he saw a teacher dressed in a mortar-board cap, black gown – the way teachers dressed a hundred years ago! He was too frightened to speak, and did as he was told. What he saw in the classroom was even worse: thirty children in Victorian clothes all sitting in neat rows. He was right. This was a haunted school, and these children were all ghosts!

'Sit down!' snapped his teacher.

It was all too much for Simon. He ran to the open window and shouted, 'Mum, come back! The school's full of Victorian ghosts!'

Then he felt a hand on his shoulder. Trembling he turned round. It was the teacher.

'Don't be frightened,' he said in a kind voice. 'We're having our Victorian day today as part of our history project!'

◀ Leave out the last two lines and write a different ending to the story, including several lines of dialogue. Use the back of this sheet.

Dear helper

Objective: To understand how speech is set out and punctuated.

Task: Ask your child to read the passage aloud to you. Help them to identify and highlight indented lines, speech marks and other punctuation using different colour pens. Discuss ideas for continuing the story.

NARRATIVE

Name

Date

The Piano: setting

◢ Think about the different scenes and events that occur in the film *The Piano.*

◢ Consider how the director sets the scene and creates a mood with only a few objects – a toy horse, a wall and so on.

◢ Which objects or people would you use to convey the right mood for the words below? Draw some ideas next to each one.

Sadness	Anger
Joy	Friendship
War	Love

Dear helper

Objective: To choose images to set a scene.

Task: Encourage your child to suggest objects that could convey the words above in a film. Discuss their ideas – do the objects create the right mood and atmosphere? Ask them to give reasons for their choices. If you would like to watch the short film *The Piano* with your child, it can be downloaded from www.aidangibbons.com/piano.html.

Name   Date

The Piano: characters

◖ Think about the main character we see in *The Piano.* Consider what he is thinking and how he may be feeling.

◖ Write down your ideas in the thought bubbles below.

Image © 2007, Aidan Gibbons.

Dear helper

Objective: To explore characters within a film.

Task: Talk about the character with your child and what they feel about him. If you would like to watch the short film *The Piano* with your child, it can be downloaded from www.aidangibbons.com/piano.html.

NARRATIVE

Name   Date

The Piano: relationships

◼ Think about the characters you see in the film *The Piano.* Choose two of them.

◼ Use the template below to write a section of dialogue between them. What do you know about them? What might they be talking about? Who might they be talking about?

A:	
B:	
A:	
B:	
A:	
B:	

Image © 2007 Aidan Gibbons

Dear helper
Objective: To show a relationship through dialogue.
Task: Your child will need to appreciate that dialogue does not need to be as detailed as a narrative, as the picture tells some of the story in film. The important thing in this activity is that they understand that dialogue can tell us a lot about what people feel about each other. Read the dialogue through with your child and encourage them to make adjustments based on what they feel works and what doesn't. If you would like to watch the short film *The Piano* with your child, it can be downloaded from www.aidangibbons.com/piano.html.

PHOTOCOPIABLE 📖SCHOLASTIC
www.scholastic.co.uk

Name   Date

Camera angles

■ Choose a scene in your house or garden and use the viewfinder to try out different angles or shots.

■ Choose three shots that best represent the scene you have chosen. Remember to think about close-ups, wide views, different angles and what you are showing in each shot – people, objects, setting.

■ Sketch each shot and write notes below.

Type of shot: _____

Brief description: _____

Type of shot: _____

Brief description: _____

Type of shot: _____

Brief description: _____

Dear helper
Objective: To see how camera angles work in a film.
Task: Reinforce the idea that the same scene looked at from different angles or viewpoints can have different effects. Play with the viewfinder and talk about the best shots your child comes up with.

NARRATIVE

Name   Date

Dialogue

■ Think about a film or TV series that you have seen and know well. Can you write a 60-second voice-over to persuade people to watch it? Think carefully about the main storyline, the characters, significant events, humour and so on. When you have finished, try out your voice-over on someone at home!

Tip:
Use short sentences to make the voice-over easy to follow.

Illustrations © Phil Garner/Beehive Illustration.

Dear helper
Objective: To write a short voice-over to summarise a story.
Task: If possible, look at some film trailers at the start of DVDs and talk about their features with your child. Encourage them to use these ideas in their own trailer. Be the audience when the trailer is finished!

Name   Date

Lights, camera, action!

◼ Today you are a film director! Think of an idea for a short story or a sequence of action that would look good on film or television. Decide what sequence of shots you would use to show this. Draw your ideas and add any director's notes in the spaces provided below.

Notes:	Notes:

Notes:	Notes:

Notes:	Notes:

Dear helper
Objective: To plan a storyboard for their own story.
Task: Talk about the ideas for the storyboard that your child may have and make suggestions if necessary. Give them positive and constructive feedback as they put the storyboard together.

Name   Date

Except after c

Write **ie** when the sound is long **e** (**ee**) except after **c**, when you should write **ei**.

Examples: **chief, field, shield, ceiling, deceive, receive**

Exceptions: **either, neither, seize**

Write **ei** when the sound is not long **e**, especially when the sound is long **a** (**ay**).

Examples: **eight, freight, height, neighbour, reign, weigh**

Exceptions: **friend, mischief**

◢ Add **ie** or **ei** in the gaps below.

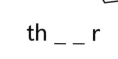

th _ _ r

ach _ _ ve

bes _ _ ge

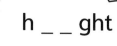

h _ _ ght

p _ _ rce

rel _ _ f

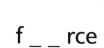

f _ _ rce

gr _ _ f

rec _ _ ve

s_ _ ze

c _ _ ling

w _ _ gh

_ _ ght

f _ _ ld

_ _ ther

Extension

◢ Choose three of the words and use them in a sentence. You can write them on the back of this sheet.

Dear helper

Objective: To learn spelling rules about words containing 'ie' or 'ei'.

Task: Help your child to write 'ie' or 'ei' in the gaps in the words above. If your child is not sure about any words, do not give the answer, but go over the rule and its exceptions and then ask your child to try again.

Name	Date

Are we agreed?

Singular subjects require singular verbs – for example, **the dog barks**.

Plural subjects take plural verbs – **the dogs bark**.

When this is done correctly, the subject (the noun or noun phrase) and verb (action word) are said to **agree**.

> **Tip:** Think hard about whether the subject of the sentence is **singular** (one) or **plural** (more than one) – **a box of tools** is singular, because it is the **box** that is the subject, not the tools.

◾ Underline the correct verb in each of these sentences.

1. The children (**look/looks**) tired.

2. This letter from the headteacher (**explain/explains**) the new school rules.

3. The exhibition of children's writing (**is/are**) in the hall.

4. The exhibition of children's art and pottery (**is/are**) in the foyer.

5. One of the computers (**has/have**) been sent back to be repaired.

6. The distress rockets fired from the *Titanic* (**was/were**) seen by the *Californian's* officer on watch.

7. The price of the CDs (**was/were**) too high.

8. This box of chocolates (**was/were**) a gift.

9. Carelessness in the use of tools (**cause/causes**) most of the accidents in design and technology lessons.

10. Tim, as well as Tom, Judy and Trudy, (**has/have**) decided to join the choir.

Dear helper

Objective: To ensure agreement between nouns and verbs.

Task: Agreement in language is about how words and phrases are used together consistently. Most of us can hear whether something 'sounds' right or wrong. So, encourage your child to say the words aloud when reading and writing. Difficulties may arise with subjects which are singular, but sound as if they are plural – a *box* of *chocolates* (the subject is *box* which is singular, not *chocolates* which is plural).

NARRATIVE

Name	Date

Computer kids

■ Read the playscript below and highlight some examples of the following: **cast list, scene descriptions, performance notes in brackets, text in italics, character names, colons, lines of dialogue.**

Cast: Mr Beetham (the class teacher); The Improvers Group of pupils: Ryan, Robert, Tracy, Trudy; Mrs Scratchit (the headmistress).

Scene 1: *Mr Beetham's classroom. On the teacher's desk is a gleaming new computer. The Improvers Group are gathered around the table.*

Mr Beetham:	Today we are going to have our first lesson in... er... ICT.
Robert:	What's that, Sir?
Tracy:	(*Hissing with scorn*) Computers, idiot!
Trudy:	Sir, I didn't know you were an expert in computers!
Mr Beetham:	(*Uncertainly*) Well, Mrs Scratchit said that I had to get myself up to date. She sent me on a computer course so that I could teach you lot all about them.

Mr Beetham starts his lesson. After much fiddling around, he manages to switch the computer on. The computer boots up and the screen fills with icons.

Mr Beetham:	Now, I've stuck the boot in – I mean, booted up. The next step is to take the... er... moose.
All:	MOUSE!
Mr Beetham:	(*Jumping up and looking round*) Where! (*Then realising his mistake*) Take the... er ... mouse... and point it at the er...
Tracy:	Icon?
Mr Beetham:	Er... icon... yes. Then... er... why is nothing happening?
Ryan:	You have to click it, Sir.
Trudy:	Double-click it.

Mr Beetham taps the mouse with his fingernail. The Improvers Group groan.

Robert:	Like this, Sir. (*He takes over.*) Then the program opens. This is a word processor.
Tracy:	The next thing is to enter text, like this. (*She types.*)
Trudy:	You can cut and paste. (*She demonstrates.*)
Ryan:	You can even add graphics. (*He demonstrates.*)

At that moment, Mrs Scratchit walks into the classroom.

Mrs Scratchit:	Well, Mr Beetham, I must compliment you on the progress of your pupils. You didn't need to go on that course after all. You are obviously an expert in computers!

Dear helper
Objective: To understand features of playscripts.
Task: Read this play with your child. You could each take several parts. Help to identify the features.

PHOTOCOPIABLE 🔲**SCHOLASTIC**
www.scholastic.co.uk

Name   Date

A mummers' play

Mummers' plays developed from oral story-telling and were one of the earliest forms of performance plays. They are simple plays about good and evil, and life and death. They were often performed at ceremonies to hasten the end of winter and cheer on the spring.

◾ Read this scene and prepare it for performance. Concentrate on speaking the lines realistically. Memorise your part if you can. Think about how you would present it on stage.

Presenter: I open the door, I enter in;
I hope your favour we shall win.
Stir up the fire and strike a light,
And see my merry boys act to-night.
Whether we stand or whether we fall,
We'll do our best to please you all.

[Enter the actors.]

Presenter: Room, room, brave gallants all,
Pray give us room to rhyme;
We're come to show activity,
This merry Christmas time;
Activity of youth,
Activity of age,
The like was never seen
Upon a common stage.
And if you don't believe what I say,
Step in St George – and clear the way.

[St George steps forward.]

St George: In come I, St George,
The man of courage bold;
With my broad axe and sword
I won a crown of gold.
I fought the fiery dragon,
And drove him to the slaughter,
And by these means I won
The King of Egypt's daughter.
Show me the man that bids me stand;
I'll cut him down with my courageous hand.

Presenter: Step in, Bold Slasher.

[Bold Slasher steps forward.]

Slasher: In come I, the Turkish Knight,
Come from the Turkish land to fight.
I come to fight St George,
The man of courage bold;
And if his blood be hot,
I soon will make it cold.

St George: Stand off, stand off, Bold Slasher,
And let no more be said,
For if I draw my sword,
I'm sure to break thy head.
Thou speakest very bold,
To such a man as I;
I'll cut thee into eyelet holes,
And make thy buttons fly.

Slasher: My head is made of iron,
My body is made of steel,
My arms and legs of beaten brass;
No man can make me feel.

St George: Then draw thy sword and fight,
Or draw thy purse and pay;
For satisfaction I must have,
Before I go away.

Slasher: No satisfaction shalt thou have,
But I will bring thee to thy grave.

St George: Battle to battle with thee I call,
To see who on this ground shall fall.

Slasher: Battle to battle with thee I pray,
To see who on this ground shall lay.

St George: Then guard thy body and
thy mind,
Or else my sword shall strike thee dead.

Slasher: One shall die and the other shall live;
This is the challenge that I do give.

[They fight. Slasher falls.]

Dear helper
Objective: To read, rehearse and perform poetry.
Task: Read this poetic play with your child, then help them to prepare for a performance – for example, by learning one of the parts and thinking about how it might be staged.

NARRATIVE

Name   Date

Bedtime blues

- Turn this dialogue into a playscript.
- Add notes to help with the production of the scene.

 Remember! Use all the appropriate conventions: cast list, scene descriptions, performance notes in brackets.

"Time for bed, Trevor," said Mrs Trubb.
"Aw, Mum, can't I stay up a bit longer?" said Trevor.
"No you can't! It's school tomorrow."
"But Trish is still up."
"I'm older than you. I'm allowed to stay up 'til ten," said Trish.
"What about Dad? He stays up really late!"
"That's because I'm on the 4 o'clock shift," snapped Dad.
"You're lucky!"
"No, I'm not. Shift work is exhausting. You want to get yourself a good education so that you can work proper hours."
"Come on, Trevor," said Mum.
"Can I listen to my CD player in bed, then?"
"He shouldn't be listening to his CDs – he hasn't even done his homework yet," said Trish.
"What!" screamed Dad.
"Well, Trevor," said Mum, "it looks like you'll be staying up later after all!"
"No, please, Mum – I'm really tired!"
"Come on, Trevor. What have you got to do?"
"History," said Trish.
"Be quiet!" snapped Trevor.
"Get your books out."
"Mum, I'm tired. I should be in bed! I've got school tomorrow."
"There!" said Trish, "I've put all his books on the table!"
"You!" hissed Trevor.
"That'll teach you to stay up past your bedtime!" said Trish.

Dear helper
Objective: To write a playscript including production notes, from a given conversation.
Task: Read through the dialogue and help your child to rewrite it as a play. Don't forget to add scene descriptions and indicate how lines should be spoken. If available, use a playscript as a model.

PHOTOCOPIABLE **SCHOLASTIC**
www.scholastic.co.uk

Name   Date

Sickly soup

■ Take two simple sentences and try
re-ordering them in different ways, as shown below.

Two simple sentences	Effect of the changes
The witch offered Amy some soup. Amy felt sick.	These could be two unrelated sentences. Amy might have felt sick for any reason.
Re-ordered	
The witch offered Amy some soup and she felt sick.	The two sentences are joined into one. 'Amy' from the second sentence is changed to the pronoun 'she' to avoid repetition.
When the witch offered Amy some soup, she felt sick.	The word 'when' emphasises that it was the offer of soup that made Amy feel sick.
Amy felt sick because the witch offered her some soup.	As above, but switching the clauses, places the emphasis on Amy rather than the witch.

■ Experiment with the following simple sentences in the same way as the
example above.

Tim ran as fast as he could. Tim missed the bus.

Tara flicked through all 30 channels. There was nothing worth watching.

It was dark. The numerals on the clock glowed faintly.

Sam failed the test. He did not revise.

It rained. They got wet.

Dear helper
Objective: To re-order and combine simple sentences.
Task: It is important for the children to understand how sentences can be re-ordered and combined.
Help your child to re-order the simple sentences above. If they get stuck, suggest using conjunctions
(joining words) such as: *although, and, as, because, but, for, until, when, where, while.*

Name   Date

Verb to noun

Verbs (action words) can often be changed to **nouns** (naming words) by changing the endings.

▪ Choose endings from the list below to change the verbs in the first column into nouns. Note that you may need to adapt the spelling when adding the ending – for example, **occupy – occupier**.

al	ar	er	or	tion
ance	ation	ment	y	

Verb	Noun
act	actor
adopt	
advertise	
amuse	
appear	
approve	
attend	
attract	
beg	
begin	
civilise	
clean	
create	
discover	
invent	
learn	
occupy	
punish	
select	
teach	

Extension

▪ Choose three verbs and write pairs of sentences showing how they can be used as verbs and nouns. You can use the back of this sheet.

Illustrations © Phil Garner/Beehive Illustration

Dear helper
Objective: To change verbs to nouns.
Task: Ask your child to read the words aloud, trying different endings until they find the one that sounds right. If in doubt, check in a dictionary.

Noun to verb

Nouns (naming words) can often be changed to **verbs** (action words) by:

1. taking off an ending – for example, **actor – act**;
2. adding an ending – for example, **memory – memorise**;
3. changing the word – for example, **blood – bleed**.

■ Change the **nouns** in the first column into **verbs** and write them in the second column. In the last column, say which method you used to make the change, using one of the numbers above.

Noun	Verb	Method
actor	act	1
apology		
amazement		
blood		
circulation		
civilisation		
composition		
computer		
description		
economy		
education		
electricity		
magnet		
memory		
national		
obedience		
purity		
relief		
solution		
song		

Extension

■ Choose three nouns and write pairs of sentences showing how they can be used as nouns and verbs. You can use the back of this sheet.

Dear helper

Objective: To change nouns to verbs.

Task: Ask your child to read the words aloud, trying different endings until they find the one that sounds right. If in doubt, check in a dictionary.

Name   Date

Drawing instructions

◼ Look at the picture below very carefully.

◼ Give a friend or a member of your family a pencil and some paper but do not let them see the picture.

◼ Describe the picture to them a bit at a time to see if they can draw the picture just from your instructions. You will need to think about the information you give them. They will need to know where to draw things and what size to draw them. You may need to use words or phrases like:

beside	above	in between	next to	the same as

◼ When you have finished, look at their picture and see how similar it is to the one above. Give yourself marks out of ten for how good your instructions were. Try it out on someone else.

Dear helper
Objective: To give verbal instructions to help someone else draw a picture.
Task: The aim of this activity is to help your child understand the importance of giving clear instructions. Discrepancies between the two pictures will help your child to see where their instructions could have been improved.

Name	Date

Helpline!

◢ You are a telephone helpline assistant who advises other people on how to go about tidying their bedrooms and keeping them tidy!

◢ Jot down some top tips that you could give people when they call.

◢ Think of some questions you would need to ask them to find out exactly what advice they need. Write them down in the best order.

◢ Try out your ideas by acting out a conversation with your helper.

NON-FICTION

Top tips	**Questions**

Illustrations © Phil Garner/Beehive Illustration.

Dear helper
Objective: To practise giving verbal instructions.
Task: Join in with your child as they practise giving verbal instructions. Take turns so they can see how others go about the task, too.

Name		Date

Video phone

- Act out making a video phone call by following the instructions below.
- Underline the **imperative** forms of the verb.
- Write instructions for using an object, such as a fire extinguisher.

DO NOT TRY TO MAKE A VIDEO CALL TO A PERSON WHO DOES NOT HAVE A VIDEO PHONE.

VIDEO

AUDIO

① **SELECT VIDEO OR AUDIO.**

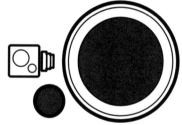

② **INSERT 20p, 50p, £1 OR £2 COINS (50p MINIMUM), OR SWIPE YOUR CREDIT CARD THROUGH THE SLOT.**

③ **DIAL THE NUMBER.**

④ **IF YOU ARE MAKING A VIDEO CALL, MAKE SURE YOU LOOK DIRECTLY AT THE CAMERA (MARKED WITH A BLACK BUTTON).**

⑤ **WHEN YOU HEAR A SERIES OF BEEPS, INSERT MORE COINS OR END YOUR CONVERSATION.**

⑥ **PRESS THE WHITE BUTTON FOR A RECEIPT AFTER A CREDIT CARD CALL.**

Dear helper

Objective: To identify the imperative form (direct order) in instructions.

Task: Help your child to role play making the call. Do this by pretending to be on the receiving end. Help your child to identify the imperative verb. Remind your child that imperative sentences give orders and usually begin with the verb that commands.

Name   Date

Instruction test drive

◖ Carefully read these instructions on how to clean your teeth.

Get your toothbrush.

Turn the tap on.

Brush your teeth.

Rinse your brush.

Wash your mouth out.

Rinse the sink.

Put toothbrush away.

◖ Follow these instructions **exactly**. Is this how you brush your teeth? Is there anything missing from the list? Add notes and comments to the instructions.

◖ Make some improvements to the instructions so they are more accurate. Then test again. Keep trying to improve the instructions until they are perfect.

New improved instructions: How to clean your teeth

NON-FICTION

Dear helper

Objective: To test a set of instructions.

Task: Join in with testing the instructions. Encourage your child to decide how effective the instructions are by talking about possible improvements based on what happened when you followed them. You could point out things like the tap should be the cold one and that the tap should be turned off during brushing!

Name   Date

NON-FICTION

Paper planes

◖ Make a paper plane. If possible, ask someone else to make one too to see if they make it the same way as you do.

◖ Make another plane, but this time, as you make it, try to write down some instructions for someone who has never made a paper plane before. You could do this on rough paper.

◖ When you have finished, follow your own instructions carefully to really test them. Have you included enough information? Are your instructions clear? Add in any additional information then write out your finished instructions here.

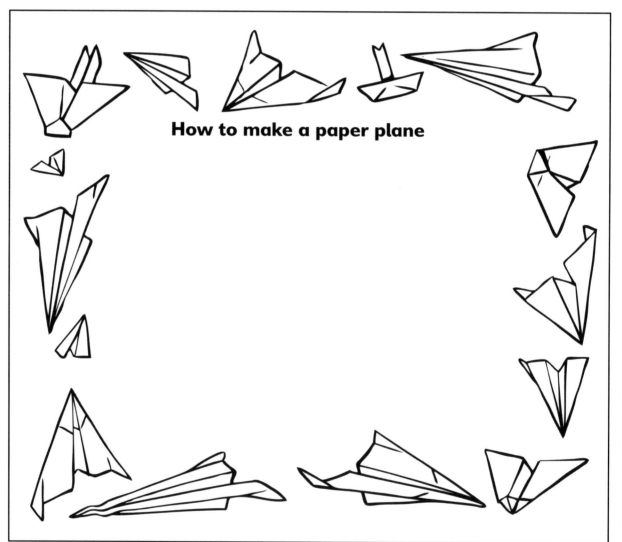

How to make a paper plane

Illustrations © Phil Garner/Beehive Illustration.

Dear helper
Objective: To write instructions for other people.
Task: Help your child to make a paper plane and then encourage them to break down the task into separate instructions. You could offer to try out the finished instructions they come up with.

Name   Date

Illustrations © Phil Garner/Beehive Illustration.

Fun and games

■ Imagine you are creating a website about the game 'Hide and seek'. On the template below, write clear instructions about how to play the game.

■ Think about what other information you could give people about the game – good places to play, history, alternative rules and so on. Decide what you would like to include on your website and add links to the boxes.

Add extra boxes, bubbles or stars as links if you wish.

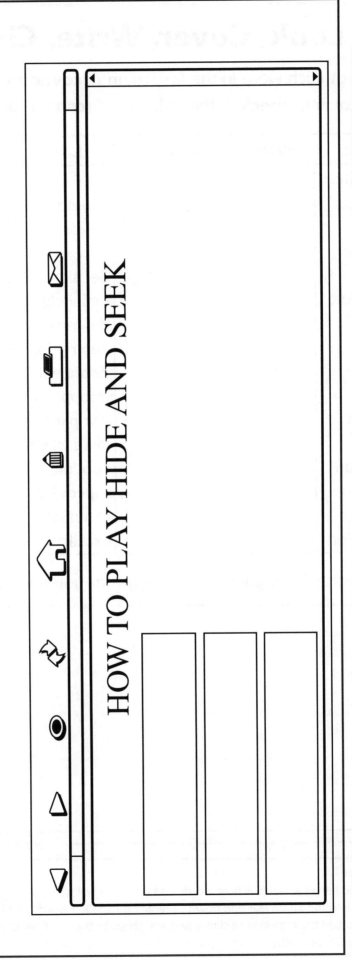

HOW TO PLAY HIDE AND SEEK

Dear helper
Objective: To plan a web page about a popular playground game.
Task: Read your child's instructions for the game and encourage them to think about the person who will carry out the instructions – you could volunteer! Talk about the layout of their instructions – for example, whether diagrams or bullet points may help and the presentation of the web page.

NON-FICTION

Look, Cover, Write, Check (1)

■ **Look** at each word in the first column, **cover** it up, **write** it in the second column, **check** it, then place a ✓ (correct) or a ✗ (wrong) after it.

Look	Write and Check	Look	Write and Check
abbreviation		convenient	
acceptable		courageous	
achieve		criticism	
amusement		deceive	
already		decision	
appropriate		definitely	
August		describe	
beautiful		description	
bicycle		disappear	
biscuit		disappoint	
breakfast		discipline	
brought		dissatisfied	
calculation		enough	
catalogue		especially	
ceiling		essential	
competition		excellent	

■ Add words from your own writing that you need to learn.

Dear helper
Objective: To keep individual lists of words and learn to spell them.
Task: Your child should be learning how to identify misspelled words and make lists of words to learn. Help them to find their spelling mistakes and add them to the list. Check that your child uses the Look, Cover, Write, Check method.

CORE SKILLS

All in a good clause (1)

Adjective clauses act like **adjectives**; they give more information about **nouns**. They are usually introduced by the following relative pronouns: **who**, **whom**, **whose**, **which**, **that**.

■ Choose a **relative pronoun** from the list above to link the **nouns** and **adjective clauses** in the boxes below. The first one has been done for you.

Noun (in bold)	Relative pronoun	Adjective clause
This is the **programme**	that	I told you about.
Cabot is the **explorer**		discovered Newfoundland.
I wish to see the **boy**		football boots were left in the classroom.
Please upgrade the **computers**		are in the computer room.
This is for the **girl**		lost her history book.
It is different from the **school**		I went to last year.
The telescope is an **instrument**		makes it possible to see distant planets.
In the room there was a **girl**		was playing with a dog.
Kari was a new **pupil**		childhood had been spent in Kosovo.
Iceland is a **country**		is north of Scotland.

Dear helper

Objective: To investigate clauses by understanding how they are connected.

Task: Though the terminology is difficult, the task is quite easy. Don't worry if your child doesn't immediately start to use the correct terminology. Ask your child to read the two clauses and try out different relative pronouns until they find one that sounds right.

CORE SKILLS

Name	Date

TV talk

■ Watch a TV programme that has an interview in it. It could be any programme where guests appear – a topical news or sports show, a music programme or a chat show.

■ Fill in the information table below about the interview.

Programme
Interviewer
Interviewee
Location (for example – in a studio, outside 10 Downing Street)
Topic/subject (for example – sport, film, news)
A good question that was asked
What did you find out?
Did you enjoy the interview? Why?
Marks out of 10

NON-FICTION

Name	Date

NON-FICTION

Order please!

◼ Read the recount below, which has been printed in the incorrect order.
Cut out the sections and arrange the paragraphs in the correct order.

✂

It was the best we'd ever had, deep and warm and dry. I could not sleep though. I lay there that night, knowing how a hunted fox must feel lying low in his lair with the hounds waiting for him outside.

    I am on stand-to the next morning, locked inside my gas mask in a world of my own, listening to myself breathing. The mist rises over no-man's-land. I see in front of me a blasted wasteland.

There was a sickly-sweet stench about the place that had to be more than stagnant mud and water. I knew well enough what it was, we all did, but no one dared speak of it. Word came back that from now on we should keep our heads down because here was where we could be most easily spotted by their snipers. But there was at least some consolation when we reached the dugout.

He is one of ours, or was. I look up where he is pointing. There are birds up there, and they are singing. I see a beady-eyed blackbird singing to the world from his barbed-wire perch. He has no tree to sing from.

No vestige of fields or trees here, not a blade of grass – simply a land of mud and craters. I see unnatural humps scattered over there beyond our wire. They are the unburied, some in field-grey uniforms and some in khaki. There is one lying in the wire with his arm stretched heavenwards, his hand pointing.

But when we got there the trenches were a bitter disappointment to us. Wilkie would have been appalled at the state of them. In places they were little more than shallow dilapidated ditches affording us precious little protection, and the mud here was even deeper than before.

Extract from Private Peaceful *by Michael Morpurgo.*

◼ Read through the text to check that the order makes sense then stick the paragraphs onto a separate sheet of paper.

Text extracts © 2003, Michael Morpurgo.

Dear helper
Objective: To understand that a recount is written in chronological order.
Task: Share the text with your child and talk about how it should be arranged.

Name	Date

NON-FICTION

Lusitania recount

◢ Using different coloured pens, highlight or underline the following features in this **recount** text: **introduction**, **chronological order**, **past tense**, **temporal connectives (linking words to do with time)**, **action focused**.

◢ Complete one feature at a time.

The *Lusitania* disaster of 1915 was like an action replay of the *Titanic* disaster of three years earlier. The two ships even looked alike, both having four tall funnels and two tall masts fore and aft.

The *Lusitania* sailed from New York to Liverpool with a full load of passengers, including Canadian soldiers, and a cargo of munitions. She was the largest liner afloat at the time (though smaller than the *Titanic*). She was also the holder of the transatlantic speed record. She was much faster than any German U-boat so it was believed that if she kept moving, there would be little danger. Just after 2:00 pm on May 7, the ship changed course toward the Irish Sea and the coast of Ireland came into view. Suddenly, a warning was shouted from the bridge, 'There is a torpedo coming, Sir!'

Soon after, there was a violent explosion in the *Lusitania* hull. It was a direct hit from a German submarine about 700 yards away. The ship sank so quickly that most lifeboats could not be lowered in time. Within 18 minutes the liner had gone down. 1198 of the 1959 passengers died – almost as many as died in the *Titanic* disaster.

The German captain, after watching the disaster through his periscope, wrote in his log, 'The ship stops immediately and quickly heels to starboard. Great confusion…Lifeboats being cleared and lowered to water. Many boats crowded…immediately fill and sink.'

The German government said that the ship had been sunk because it was carrying soldiers and munitions. However, public opinion was outraged, and it was one of the reasons why America eventually joined the war against Germany.

Extension

◢ The extract from the German captain's log book is different in style. What are the differences? (**Hint!** Look for tense and sentence structure.)

Illustrations © Phil Garner/Beehive Illustration.

Dear helper
Objective: To identify the features of recount texts.
Task: Remind your child that a recount is a text that is written to retell for information or entertainment. Read the text with your child, then help them to find and highlight examples of the different features.

Name   Date

Said

Said is a word that we use a lot in our writing but there are better, more effective words that we can use instead. Words that describe how we say things and tell the reader how we might be feeling are often better.

■ In the word **said** below collect words that can be used instead of said. Try to include some **'wow'** words that are really effective.

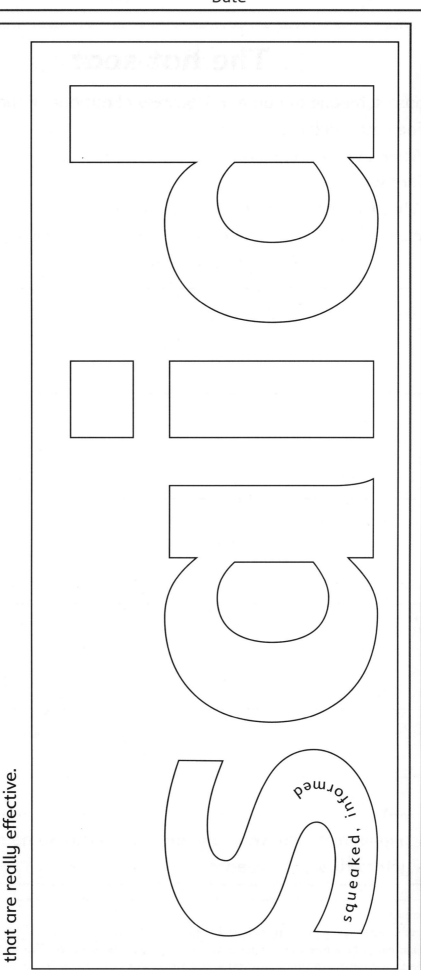

Dear helper
Objective: To be aware of the alternatives to *said*.
Task: Help your child to collect suitable words that could be used instead of *said* in their writing.

NON-FICTION

Name   Date

NON-FICTION

The hot-seat

- Choose someone at home to interview about one of these topics.
  - ☐ The best holiday ever!
  - ☐ When I was at school
  - ☐ That was funny!
  - ☐ What I wanted to be when I was young
- Plan some questions in the boxes below. Think carefully about what you want to find out and the best way to ask.

1.
2.
3.
4.
5.

- When you are happy with your questions, make some notes under each one as you carry out the interview.

Dear helper
Objective: To interview another person and collect information.
Task: Volunteer to be interviewed or suggest someone else who could be. Talk about the questions beforehand and then discuss what was found out afterwards.

PHOTOCOPIABLE SCHOLASTIC

www.scholastic.co.uk

Name	Date

Newfoundland notes

- Read this description of Newfoundland.
- Make notes using the format below which is designed to stop you writing full sentences.
- Look at the map and make a few notes.
- Write a short paragraph from your notes. Use the back of the sheet.

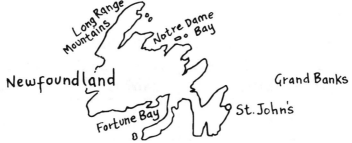

The Vikings were the first to discover this large island in about the year 1000. They called it Vinland. In 1497, the island was rediscovered by John Cabot, who called it the 'new foundelande'. Nearly one hundred years later, in 1583, England claimed it as its first overseas colony. At that time St John's, now the capital city, was a flourishing settlement. The city is near to the Grand Banks, which are the world's richest fishing grounds, and has the best natural harbour in the country. In 1948, Newfoundland voted to join Canada as its tenth province.

The island has an area of 156,185 square miles and a population of approximately 600,000. The lowest average temperature in the St John's area is –30.3°C in January, and the highest is 16.2°C. More than 90% of the land area is covered by forest. The main industries are forestry and fishing.

Notes (words or phrases)	Numbers (where appropriate)
Discovered by Vikings	About 1000

Dear helper

Objective: To make notes and build on these in writing.

Task: Encourage your child to read the text and study the map. Check that the notes in the first column are words and phrases only, not full sentences.

NON-FICTION

Name   Date

Abbreviations

Abbreviations are useful in note-taking and many are accepted in ordinary texts. Note that full stops are often used after abbreviations, though they are omitted in very common abbreviations, such as Mr, Dr and BBC.

■ Write the meaning of the **abbreviations** (Abbr.) in the **meanings** column. The first one is done for you.

■ Try to find more abbreviations and write them on the back of this sheet.

Abbr.	Meanings	Abbr.	Meanings
&	and	km	
£		Mon.	
Ave.		Mr	
BA		Ms	
BBC		pm	
Beds.		Rd	
Blvd.		Sgt.	
cm		SOS	
Co.		St.	
DJ		UHF	
Dr		vol.	
FM		YHA	
g		Yorks.	

Dear helper
Objective: To use simple abbreviations.
Task: Help your child find the meanings of the more difficult abbreviations by using a dictionary. Then, encourage your child to find more examples of abbreviations, preferably used in a real context, such as newspapers and magazines.

PHOTOCOPIABLE SCHOLASTIC
www.scholastic.co.uk

Beautiful

Words ending in **consonant + y** change the **y** to **i** before adding any suffix not beginning with **i** – for example, **friendly** + **er** = **friendlier**; **busy** + **ly** = **busily**.

◼ Fill in the **New word** column, making sure that you follow the rules.

Root	Suffix	New word
beauty	ful	beautiful
busy	ly	
carry	er	
empty	ing	
friendly	est	
glory	fy	
happy	ness	
hungry	est	
lazy	ly	
marry	age	
mercy	less	
merry	est	
pity	ful	
pretty	ness	
reply	cate	
spy	ing	
supply	ed	
try	al	
vary	able	
windy	ly	

Dear helper
Objective: To learn the spelling rule about words ending in 'y', when adding a suffix.
Task: Remind your child that a suffix is a group of letters added to the end of a word to change its meaning or use. Ask your child to read each word aloud and then look carefully at the suffix to see how to apply the rule.

CORE SKILLS

Name Date

Hallucinate

Dictionaries contain a range of information about words. Here is a typical dictionary entry, followed by an explanation of the information it contains.

hallucinate (ha-loó-si-nate) *v.* false impressions in the mind.
[*L. alucinari* wander in mind]

- ☐ **Spelling:** the bold print word at the beginning of the entry shows the spelling.
- ☐ **Pronunciation:** how a word should be pronounced, usually by re-spelling the word phonetically.
- ☐ **Part of speech:** this is shown by abbreviations like the following:

noun *n.*	adjective *adj.*
verb *v.*	preposition *prep.*
adverb *adv.*	conjunction *conj.*

- ☐ **Meaning:** this is the main purpose of the standard dictionary. Words with several meanings have long entries.
- ☐ **Etymology** word origin: An abbreviation showing from which language the word comes. Common abbreviations are: *F.* French, *G.* Greek, *Ger.* German, *Goth.* Gothic, *L.* Latin, *ME.* Middle English, *ON.* Old Norse.

■ Find the answers to the following questions using your dictionary.

1. Is it correct to pronounce the **h** in **honour**?
2. What does the abbreviation **CBI** stand for?

3. What does **cosmos** mean?
4. From which language does **cosmos** originally come?
5. How many different meanings can you find for the word **bill**?
6. From which language does **skirt** originally come?

7. What is the meaning of the abbreviation **NATO**?
8. How should you pronounce the word **boatswain**?

Dear helper
Objective: To understand the different purposes of a dictionary.
Task: Read through the explanation of a dictionary entry with your child, matching the features to those in the dictionary your child has brought home. Then, help them to answer the questions.

Look, Cover, Write, Check (2)

■ **Look** at each word in the first column, **cover** it up, **write** it in the second column, **check** it, then place a ✓ (correct) or a ✗ (wrong) after it.

Look	Write and Check	Look	Write and Check
except		irrelevant	
exercise		irritable	
existence		judge	
extremely		knowledge	
fought		leisure	
February		library	
government		likeable	
guard		lovable	
guess		maintain	
height		maintenance	
humorous		manageable	
humour		marriage	
immediate		minute	
immediately		mischief	
independent		misspelled	
insistent		naive	
instalment		naughty	

■ Add words from your own writing that you need to learn.

CORE SKILLS

Dear helper
Objective: To keep individual lists of words and learn to spell them.
Task: Your child should be learning how to identify misspelled words and make lists of words to learn. Help them to find their spelling mistakes and add them to the list. Check that your child uses the Look, Cover, Write, Check method.

Trudy's Dream Present

Pronouns are used in place of nouns to avoid repetition.

Personal pronouns: I, you, he, she, it, me, him, her, my, mine, your, yours, his, hers, its, we, they, us, them, our, ours, their, theirs.

 Read Version 1 of *Trudy's Dream Present*, an example of a writer not using any personal pronouns.

Version 1

Trudy got Trudy's dream present for Christmas – a mobile phone. Trudy couldn't wait to try the mobile phone out, so Trudy dialled a number. Trudy was disappointed when nothing happened. Then Trudy realised that Trudy hadn't turned the mobile phone on. Trudy flicked the switch and tried again, but again Trudy was disappointed because the mobile phone was still dead. Just then, Trudy's friend, Trisha, came into the room. Trudy told Trisha that Trudy had got a mobile phone for Christmas. "Great, so has Trisha! said Trisha. "Trudy and Trisha can call each other!" Trudy said that Trudy had tried but the mobile phone wouldn't work. Trisha asked if Trisha could have a look. Trisha looked at the battery indicator. "Trisha thought so," said Trisha. "Trudy hasn't charged the battery!"

 Now read Version 2 of *Trudy's Dream Present*, an example of a writer using too many personal pronouns.

Version 2

She got her dream present for Christmas – a mobile phone. She couldn't wait to try it out, so she dialled a number. She was disappointed when nothing happened. Then she realised that she hadn't turned it on. She flicked the switch and tried again, but again she was disappointed because the phone was still dead. Just then, her friend came into the room. She told her that she had got a mobile phone for Christmas. "Great, so have I," she said. "We can call each other!" She said that she had tried but it wouldn't work. She asked if she could have a look. She looked at the battery indicator. "I thought so," said she. "You haven't charged the battery!"

 Write your own version of *Trudy's Dream Present* with the right balance of personal pronouns and names. Use the back of this sheet or a separate piece of paper.

Illustrations © Phil Garner/Beehive Illustration

Dear helper
Objective: To revise the function of pronouns.
Task: Read through the texts with your child. Help them to make the corrections orally by using simple common sense – what sounds right. If necessary, help with producing the written version.

Achievement

Keep the final **e** before a **suffix** beginning with a consonant – for example,

hope + **ful** = **hopeful**

Exceptions: **true** + **ly** = **truly**, **argue** + **ment** = **argument**

Drop the final **e** before a **suffix** beginning with a vowel – for example,

live + **ing** = **living**

◀ Fill in the **New word** column, making sure that you follow the rules.

Root	Suffix	New word
achieve	ment	achievement
advance	ing	
approve	al	
compare	able	
continue	ing	
desire	able	
guide	ance	
hope	ful	
nine	ty	
retire	ment	
separate	ing	
severe	ly	
shame	less	
taste	ful	
true	ly	
tune	ful	
use	less	
whole	ly	

Dear helper

Objective: To learn spelling rules about words ending in 'e' when adding a suffix.

Task: Remind your child that a suffix is a group of letters added to the end of a word to change its meaning or use. Ask your child to read each word aloud and then look carefully at the suffix to see how to apply the two rules.

CORE SKILLS

Name   Date

NON-FICTION

Investigating adverts

◼ Watch some TV adverts and look at other adverts in papers and magazines.

◼ Begin to think about what makes a really effective advert and jot down your ideas in the diagram below. Add more circles if you need to.

◼ Think about colour, text, words, images, ideas and if it persuades you, how?

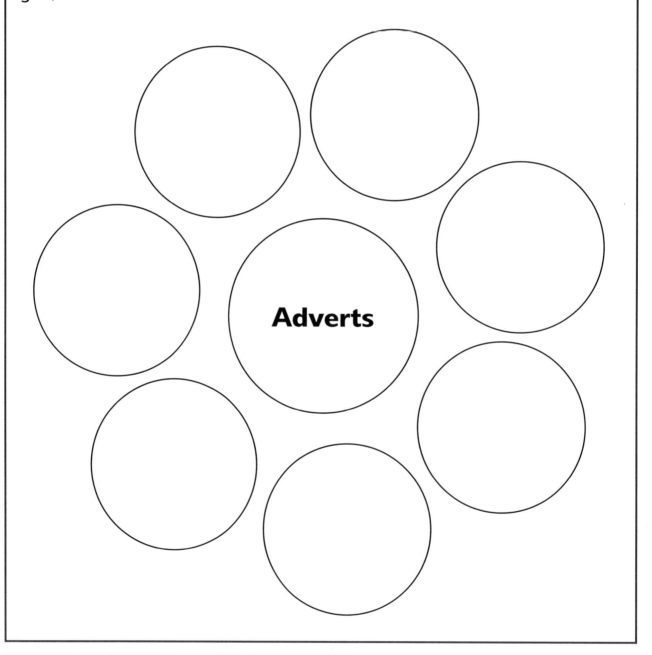

Dear helper
Objective: To identify key features of persuasive texts.
Task: Watch some TV adverts with your child and if possible share some from magazines. Together think about which ones are the most effective and why?

Name

Date

Wow words

■ Look at different forms of advertising (TV, magazine and so on) and collect some '**wow**' words and phrases that are really effective in persuading. Write them in the outline below.

Dear helper

Objective: To collect persuasive words and phrases.

Task: Share as many adverts with your child as you can and focus them on the key words or phrases that are used to persuade us.

Name   Date

What persuades us?

◼ Read the extract below. Highlight or underline the words, phrases or sentences that you feel are the most effective.

SATS (Stop Animal Testing Society) says: STOP ANIMAL TESTING

The facts

Every year in the UK over 2.7 million animals are hurt or killed in scientific tests. Official statistics show that 31% of tests are for biological research, 24% are for testing drugs and 18% are tests for the safety of foodstuffs, household products and agricultural chemicals. The remaining 27% include testing for a wide range of purposes, for example, genetic testing.

Why animal testing is wrong

First, the tests are cruel and cause animals a great deal of suffering, especially as 60% of the tests are given without any anaesthetic. Pain-relieving drugs are not usually given because experimenters claim their use would interfere with test results. Secondly, the majority of the tests are not for life-saving drugs or important medical advances, but for trivial things, such as whether a new shampoo is safe if it gets into the eyes. Of course, no one wants to be harmed by shampoo – but do we really want animals to suffer just to add another brand to the supermarket shelves?

Finally, the tests are outdated and unnecessary. Modern science offers a range of tests that are more reliable and more humane, including chemical analysis and computer models.

What you can do

Join SATS. We are a non-violent organisation working to change the law through legal means, such as raising public awareness, leafleting and political lobbying. Sign up at www.sats.org. Membership is free, though donations are welcome.

Illustrations © Phil Garner/Beehive Illustration

Dear helper
Objective: To understand the different ways authors persuade us.
Task: The important idea in this activity is that the children recognise how authors persuade in their writing. Share the text and encourage the children to look for other examples in books.

PHOTOCOPIABLE 📖SCHOLASTIC
www.scholastic.co.uk

Name

Date

NON-FICTION

One-kid crime wave

■ Find the **persuasive devices** used in this article. Use the code in brackets to mark the text at the end of the appropriate line:

- ☐ persuasive phrases such as, 'What nonsense!' (**ph**)
- ☐ specific examples (**eg**)
- ☐ facts, figures and statistics (**fa**)
- ☐ appeals to the emotion (**em**)
- ☐ appeals to what is right or fair (**ri**)
- ☐ appeals to common sense (**se**).

Young offenders need to be dealt with more severely, otherwise they will continue to break the law, and end up living a life of crime.

    An example is Ben (his real name has been changed). Local people have nicknamed him the 'one-kid crime wave'. In the year before his arrest last September he had committed 20 crimes. These included burglary, blackmail, attacking an old-age pensioner and various motor vehicle offences. Yet he was let off with a caution, or let out on bail every time he was caught.

    Social workers tried to solve Ben's problems by sending him on a two-week holiday to St Lucia, an island in the Caribbean. They say that this will help to improve his self-confidence, and set him on the right track to becoming a law-abiding citizen. How unfair! Just imagine how that poor old-age pensioner must have felt when he heard that Ben had been sent to the Caribbean!

    No one but a complete idiot would believe that this could work. It is rewarding Ben for his crimes. Now he will think that, the next time he fancies an exotic holiday, all he has to do is hit an old lady over the head!

    Every right-thinking person can see that the only way to reform boys like Ben is to punish them for their crimes. If Ben had been punished for his first crime, for example, by being sent to a young offenders secure unit for a few months, then perhaps the other 19 crimes would not have been committed.

    This is the common-sense way of dealing with young offenders which the vast majority of people support – and these are the people who pay, through taxes, for an effective system of law and order.

Illustrations © Phil Garner/Beehive Illustration.

Dear helper
Objective: To investigate the use of persuasive devices.
Task: Read the passage with your child, then help them to find the persuasive techniques used in the passage. Discuss the issue and offer your own opinions. If time allows, do the same with an article in the newspaper.

Name   Date

Fact or opinion? (1)

◾ Read the three statements below and think about the difference between fact, opinion and bias.

London is in Britain.	**FACT**
London is a lovely city.	**OPINION**
I live in London and it is the best city in the world.	**BIAS**

◾ Collect more examples of fact, opinion and bias. Write them in the table below.

Fact	Opinion	Bias

Dear helper
Objective: To identify fact, opinion and bias.
Task: Support your child in finding different examples of fact, opinion and bias by looking at newspapers, magazines, TV news and so on.

Name	Date

Fact or opinion? (2)

🔲 Read the extract below.

🔲 Highlight the sections you consider to contain facts in red and the sections that are an opinion in blue. Are there any sections that are left without highlights?

Come to Greece!
Visit the place where Western civilisation began…

Greece is amazing! Everywhere you look, the past is all around – it's like walking through history. You can go into temple courtyards and touch pillars, stones and sculptures that are 25 centuries old. You can see tiny carved jewels that were made in 400 years BC – that's more than 30 lifetimes ago!

Peaceful countryside

Amid breathtaking scenery and charming villages there are so many spectacular ruins to see. The Temple of Apollo Bassae, dedicated to the god Apollo, is hidden away miles from any town in beautiful rural Arcadia. Some historians think this temple was designed by the same architect who built the Parthenon on the Acropolis, which towers above bustling Athens. The Parthenon is still there today in this exciting capital city – so why not visit it?

Learn about life in the past

There are so many places to enjoy a glass of locally-made wine and to try the delicious traditional dishes of *souvlaki* and *moussaka*. Back in Ancient Greek times they also loved to eat and drink, as we can see in the pictures on pieces of their pottery. Look out for them in the many fascinating museums around the country.

But there's much more to Greece than history and temples!

Nestling between the Mediterranean and Aegean, it is really hot – perfect for sun worshippers. The pure sea is warm and welcoming for swimmers – can't you imagine yourself diving in? Or, if you're feeling adventurous, sail off to explore the hundreds of tiny Greek islands, like the sailors and traders of old. It's up to you, because there's something for everyone in Greece!

🔲 Could you design a similar leaflet about your town or village? Remember to try to get a balance between fact and opinion as this is the best way to persuade.

Dear helper

Objective: To investigate the balance of fact and opinion in a persuasive text.

Task: Read through this extract and help your child to consider which parts are factual and which contain opinion. There may be parts that you find difficult to classify as fact or opinion. Spend some time discussing these parts with your child but if in doubt, leave these blank for your child to discuss in class.

NON-FICTION

Name   Date

Old school fields

*In his letter below, Mr Rudge is understandably upset that new houses are going to be built nearby, but his letter of complaint is full of **bias**, **hearsay** and **deliberate misrepresentations of fact**.*

◼ Use different coloured pens to highlight all the examples of these that you can find in the letter.

◼ Write a reply to Mr Rudge from the council's point of view.

Dear Sir,

I am writing to protest about the plans for the new dwelling units in Old School Fields. Ten houses are far too many for such a tiny field. There will be terrible problems with road access. As you can see from the plan, the road will be very narrow. This will mean that it will be congested with traffic, and this will cause many accidents. It will be the children who suffer most.

A friend of mine, who is a builder, says that there is no main drain anywhere near the Old School Field, and that these houses will have to have cess tanks. That will cause a terrible smell in summer, and my wife suffers from hay fever.

Another thing is that the old school will be knocked down. The keystone over the front door says 1881. Surely this is a historic building that should be preserved? I think this is just another example of profiteering by builders. They want to knock it down so that they can squeeze in another two houses.

Also, I have heard a rumour that these houses will be used to accommodate people who have caused problems on other estates. This is a nice quiet area and we can do without those kinds of problems. If these plans go ahead, it will ruin our quality of life.

Yours faithfully,

Mr Ivor G. Rudge

KEY

◻ New Private Dwellings   ==== Drains

◻ Older houses   ⊢━⊣ Old School Fields

⊏⊐ Old School, 1901,   ◯ ◖ Traffic calming measures
restored as community centre

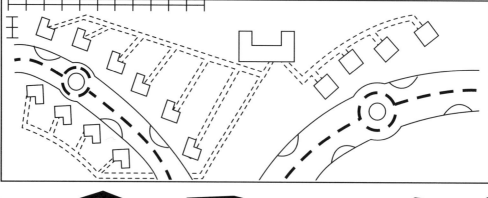

Dear helper
Objective: To recognise bias.
Task: Help your child to compare the opinions stated in the letter with the facts shown on the plan. Discuss how a council official from the planning department might reply.

Name	Date

Dear Councillor...

◼ Write a letter to your local council to suggest an improvement for the local community. This could be for specific groups (such as the under fives, teenagers, Senior Citizens) or for everyone.

◼ Begin by making some notes on why your idea is a good one, why it is needed, and what the benefits will be. Be persuasive! Use your Wow words and any other persuasive technique you know of.

◼ Copy out your letter here.

Dear

Yours sincerely,

Dear helper
Objective: To draft a letter with a real purpose.
Task: As your child plans out their letter, encourage them to focus on how they can use words, phrases or techniques to persuade the recipient of the letter.

NON-FICTION

Name   Date

Read all about it!

Congratulations – you are the new editor of *The Daily Buzz!*

◼ Your first front page is waiting for your words of wisdom below. There is a space for your headline, a photograph and your first editorial!

◼ Remember that your editorial gives your own opinion but is based on key facts.

NON-FICTION

The Daily Buzz

Dear helper
Objective: To give your personal view in a newspaper editorial.
Task: If possible look at a few editorials, or opinion pieces, from newspapers. Remind your child that the writing should be their personal view about the issue that they have been asked to write about.

PHOTOCOPIABLE ▪️SCHOLASTIC
www.scholastic.co.uk

Name	Date

Book advertisement

■ Prepare an advertisement for a book using these headings.

Title and author

Illustration (Draw your own sketch to give the reader an idea of what the book is about. Do not copy the book's cover, but think of your own idea.)

Main character (Describe what he or she is like, and what he or she does.)

Main character (Draw a simple sketch of the main character.)

Outline of story (Give an outline of the story that would interest the reader. However, be careful not to give away the ending.)

Dear helper
Objective: To persuade someone to buy a book through an advertisement.
Task: Talk about the book that your child has chosen to advertise. Discuss what he or she will write or draw.

Name   Date

NON-FICTION

Boreham Supertram

- Read the letter from Boreham Council.
- Discuss the good and bad points of the plan.

Boreham Town Hall
Boreham
BT3 TCH

4 January 2009

Residents of Boreham
All residential addresses

Dear Resident,

Boreham Council is pleased to announce plans for a modern tramway system which will be fast, economical and environmentally-friendly. A plan of the Supertram system is given below. When the tramway is completed, all cars will be banned from the town centre, and must be left at the 'Supertram parks' outside the town. Fares will be between £2 and £5 depending on the length of the journey. If you would like to send us your views about the plans, please write to me within 30 days at the address in the top right-hand corner.

Yours sincerely,

Mr Leclerk
On behalf of Boreham Council

KEY

═══ **B** roads

──── **A** roads

─ ─ ─ Proposed route of Supertram

╫╫╫╫ Railway track (disused)

P Park and ride

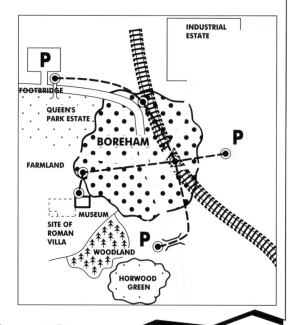

- Write a letter supporting or arguing against the plan, following the letter template. Use a separate sheet.

Dear helper
Objective: To write a letter expressing a point of view.
Task: If there is a local issue that your child could write about, use it instead of the Boreham Supertram. Ensure that your child fully understands the issue – for example, by reading a newspaper article, or by explaining it yourself. Write about the issue on another sheet of paper, following the example above.

Illustrations © Phil Garner/Beehive Illustration

PHOTOCOPIABLE 📖SCHOLASTIC
www.scholastic.co.uk

Name	Date

Uniform arguments

◼ Read the notes **for** school uniform, then in the space below, make notes **against** school uniform.

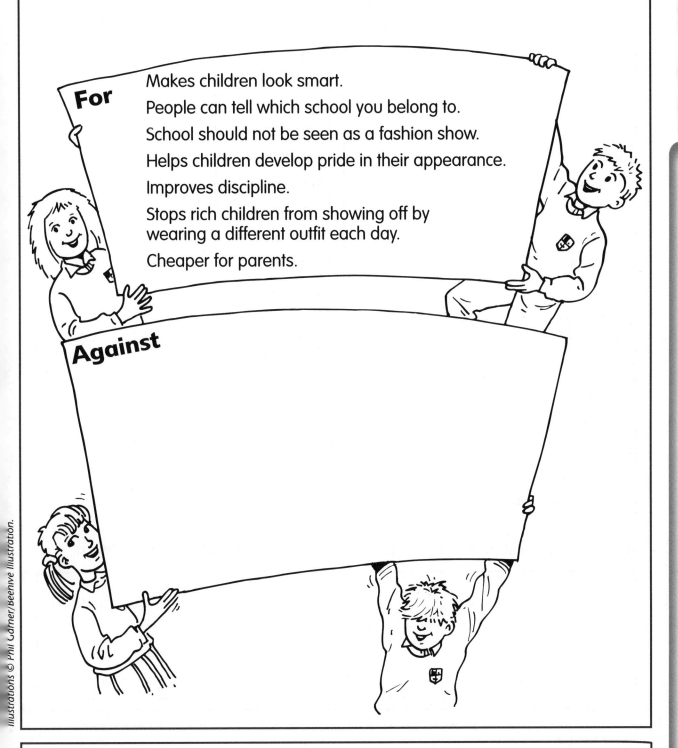

For

Makes children look smart.

People can tell which school you belong to.

School should not be seen as a fashion show.

Helps children develop pride in their appearance.

Improves discipline.

Stops rich children from showing off by wearing a different outfit each day.

Cheaper for parents.

Against

Dear helper
Objective: To construct an argument in note form.
Task: Read through the statements for school uniform with your child, then discuss the issue. This will help to give your child ideas for arguments against school uniforms.

Look, Cover, Write, Check (3)

◼ **Look** at each word in the first column, **cover** it up, **write** it in the second column, **check** it, then place a ✓ (correct) or a ✗ (wrong) after it.

Look	Write and Check	Look	Write and Check
neighbour		rhyme	
noticeable		rhythm	
occasionally		seize	
occur		separate	
once		separately	
panicked		similar	
parallel		sincerely	
patient		solemn	
possess		success	
priest		surprise	
professor		thorough	
pursue		twelfth	
queue		unnecessary	
queueing		vicious	
receive		weight	
recommend		whistle	
remember		yacht	
restaurant		yield	

◼ Add to the list words from your own writing that you need to learn.

Dear helper
Objective: To keep individual lists of words and learn to spell them.
Task: Your child should be learning how to identify misspelled words and make lists of words to learn. Help them to find their spelling mistakes and add them to the list. Check that your child uses the Look, Cover, Write, Check method.

Adjective to adverb

Adjectives (describing words) can often be changed to **adverbs** (words that describe verbs) by adding **-ly**. Note that, if the word ends in **y**, the **y** must be changed to **i** – for example, hung**ry**, hung**ri**ly.

◖ Change the **adjectives** in the first column into **adverbs**. The first one has been done for you.

Adjective	Adverb
angry	angrily
anxious	
bad	
careful	
clumsy	
correct	
greedy	
happy	
hungry	
immediate	
quiet	
serious	
sudden	
sulky	
weak	

Extension

◖ Choose three adjectives and write pairs of sentences showing how they can be used as adjectives and adverbs. Use the back of this sheet.

Dear helper
Objective: To change adjectives to adverbs.
Task: Ask your child to read the words aloud, then add '-ly', taking care with words ending in 'y'.

CORE SKILLS

Name _____ Date _____

From bad to worse

Sometimes we need to compare things.

The **positive** is used to describe something – for example, Zita is tall.

The **comparative** is used to compare two things – for example, Zita is tall but Rita is taller.

The **superlative** is used when comparing lots of things – for example, Anita is the tallest of all.

◼ Fill in the gaps in the boxes.

Positive	Comparative	Superlative
Regular with **-er**, **-est** endings		
fast small	faster taller	fastest smallest thinnest
Regular with **more** and **most**		
beautiful comfortable	more beautiful more generous	most beautiful most comfortable most intelligent
Irregular		
bad many	worse less	worst best

Extension

◼ Choose a word from each of the boxes and write sentences for each, demonstrating the use of the **positive** form, the **comparative** form and the **superlative** form. You can use the back of this sheet.

Illustrations © Phil Garner/Beehive Illustration.

Dear helper
Objective: To change adjectives to show degrees of comparison.
Task: Encourage your child to say each degree of comparison before completing the table. Remind them that *most* and '-est' should not be used together. They shouldn't, for example, say: *I am the most smartest.*

Name	Date

Poetry analyser

◼ Use this writing frame to help you write about the poem your teacher has given you.

Subject: Say briefly what the poem is about.

Theme: Explain the ideas that are expressed in the poem.

Form: Describe the form of the poem.
Is it written in verses? If so, how many lines in each verse?

What rhyme scheme is used? Write it out using letters of the alphabet.

How many stressed syllables in each line? (Count the first four lines.)

Are the lines long or short?

Is there a regular pattern?

Style: Look for unusual and interesting words. Jot some down and explain why they are effective.

Look for figures of speech, such as similes and metaphors. Write down one or two and explain them.

POETRY

Dear helper
Objective: To explore the style, form and theme of a poem.
Task: Your child should have used a writing frame like this before. Read together the poem your child has brought home. Discuss how to complete each section and share your own responses.

Name	Date

The poetry processor

Write three adjectives describing the subject of the poem.	Write three words that sum up the emotions aroused by the subject of the poem.
Write a simile to describe the subject of the poem.	Describe a landscape that would be a good backdrop for the subject of your poem.
Write a simile to describe the subject of your poem, then cross out 'like'. (You have written a metaphor!)	Write a line that contains a verb which is something the subject of your poem might do.
Talk to your subject as though it were human. (You have added personification!)	Write three adverbs to go with any of the verbs you have used.
What does the subject of your poem make you think about?	What mood does the subject of your poem put you in?
Find the best line you have written so far and repeat it.	Write a line about something which is the opposite of your subject.
Say how you feel about the subject of your poem.	If the subject of your poem were music, what would it sound like?
Write three words that you associate with the subject of your poem.	Think of something completely different to your subject and try to compare it with the subject in a simile.

● Cut out and shuffle the cards. Use them to help you to write a poem.

● Redraft your poem by choosing your best lines, placing them in the best order and writing extra lines, where necessary.

Dear helper
Objective: To write a poem conveying feelings, reflections or moods.
Task: You can help your child by making this poetry-writing game fun. Help your child with ideas. You could also help by writing a poem yourself.

Name _____ Date _____

All kinds of poems

Definitions

☐ A **clerihew** is a four-line comic poem about a person who is named in the first line.

☐ A **haiku** consists of seventeen syllables.

☐ A **limerick** is a short humorous poem with a bouncy rhythm.

☐ A **sonnet** has rhyme and fourteen lines.

☐ Many **ballads** have rhyme schemes of a b c b.

◼ Read these poems or parts of poems aloud.

◼ Write down the name of the form used in each poem. Use the definitions above to help you.

◼ Try to add more information to the definitions. Use the back of this sheet.

I sat next to a duchess at tea,
Distressed as a person could be.
Her rumblings abdominal
Were simply phenomenal
And everyone thought it was me.

Anon

Form _____

The King sits in Dumfermlin town
Drinking the blood-red wine:
'O, where will I get a skilly skipper
To sail this ship of mine?'

Anon

Form _____

Sir Francis Drake
Learned to sail on a lake –
But defeating the Armada
Was much harder!

Anon

Form _____

Earth has not anything to show more fair:
Dull would he be of soul who could pass by
A sight so touching in its majesty:
This City now doth, like a garment, wear
The beauty of the morning; silent, bare,
Ships, towers, domes, theatres, and temples lie
Open unto the fields, and to the sky;
All bright and glittering in the smokeless air.
Never did sun more beautifully steep
In his first splendour, valley, rock, or hill;
Ne'er saw I, never felt, a calm so deep!
The river glideth at his own sweet will:
Dear God! the very houses seem asleep;
And all that mighty heart is lying still!

William Wordsworth

Form _____

Storm clouds gathering
The forest sighs in the wind
A screech from a crow.

Piatto

Form _____

Dear helper

Objective: To understand terms that describe different kinds of poem.

Task: Share the reading of these poems with your child, then help them to match each one to the definitions given above.

Name	Date

Table-top planet

◼ Read this literal-figurative poem. Notice how all the phrases and sentences on the left-hand side are **literal** and all those on the right are **figurative**. The figurative statements are mostly metaphors, but there is one simile – can you find it?

Literal	Figurative
My pen is	a miniature space ship full of tiny aliens.
The top of the table is	a flat brown field on which the spaceship has landed.
This piece of paper is	a patch of cold, fresh snow.
My eraser is	the aliens' exploration vehicle.
These tiny bits left by the eraser are	the aliens exploring in their spacesuits.
The little bits are clustered round the pen.	They want to go back home to Venus where it is as hot as a pressure cooker.
The pen is empty.	But they have run out of fuel.
I'm going to throw the pen away and clean my desk.	A giant earthling wipes them out.

Illustrations © Phil Garner/Beehive Illustration.

◼ Write your own literal-figurative poem. Start with a group of everyday objects (such as the contents of your pocket or your schoolbag or what's on the dining table) and let your imagination create a new world around them.

Dear helper
Objective: To investigate and create metaphors.
Task: Although your child will have been taught the terms, remind them what *literal* (realistic, factual) and *figurative* (imaginative, symbolic) mean. Read the poem with your child, taking half-lines each. Talk about how ordinary things are transformed by imagination.

All in a good clause (2)

Adverb clauses act like adverbs; they give more information about **how**, **when**, **where** or **why**. For example, the first adverb clause in the table explains why the band could not play. Adverb clauses are usually introduced by the following **subordinating connectives**:

after, **although**, **as**, **because**, **before**, **unless**, **when**, **where**, **while**.

◼ Choose a **subordinating conjunction** from the list above to link the main clauses and adverb clauses. The first one has been done for you.

Main clause	Subordinating conjunction	Adverb clause (how, when, where, why)
The band couldn't play	because	Bill had forgotten his trombone.
We tuned up		Bill fetched his instrument.
We will not win the competition		we play our very best.
The recording sounded good		our drummer was sick.
We might even be famous		the CD is released.
We won't get into the top ten		swing music is not popular.
Don't forget to blow harder		the music should be loud.
We must tune up carefully		the concert starts.
There will be time to rest		the concert has finished.
I don't think I'll be a musician		it is too much like hard work.

Illustrations © Phil Garner/Beehive Illustration.

Dear helper

Objective: To investigate clauses by understanding how they are connected.

Task: Though the terminology is difficult, the task is quite easy. Don't worry if your child doesn't immediately start to use the correct terminology. Ask your child to read the two clauses and try out different subordinating conjunctions until they find one which sounds right. Sometimes, either of two conjunctions works equally well.

Name	Date

The Highwayman

◼ Read through the beginning of poem 'The Highwayman' shown below.

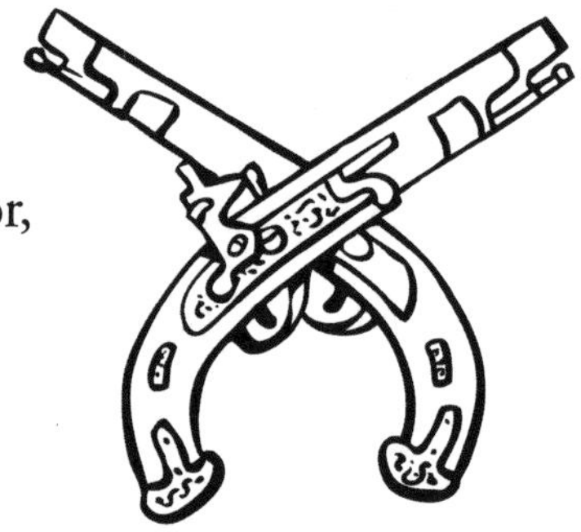

The wind was a torrent of darkness upon the gusty trees,
The moon was a ghostly galleon tossed upon cloudy seas,
The road was a ribbon of moonlight looping the purple moor,
And the highwayman came riding—
Riding—riding—
The highwayman came riding, up to the old inn door.

He'd a French cocked hat on his forehead, and a bunch of lace at his chin;
He'd a coat of the claret velvet, and breeches of fine doe-skin.
They fitted with never a wrinkle; his boots were up to his thigh!
And he rode with a jewelled twinkle—
His rapier hilt a-twinkle—
His pistol butts a-twinkle, under the jewelled sky.

Over the cobbles he clattered and clashed in the dark inn-yard,
He tapped with his whip on the shutters, but all was locked and barred,
He whistled a tune to the window, and who should be waiting there
But the landlord's black-eyed daughter—
Bess, the landlord's daughter—
Plaiting a dark red love-knot into her long black hair.

Alfred Noyes

◼ Read the verses aloud to yourself a few times. As you read think about how you say the words and how you can make the poem come to life by adding actions, movement and expression to match what is being said.

◼ Use a mirror so you can see your expression and actions as you read each verse.

◼ Ask friends or family what they think of your performance. What did they like? What did it make them feel?

Poem © 1914, Alfred Noyes; illustrations © Phil Garner/Beehive Illustration.

Dear helper
Objective: To read a poem aloud using action and expression.
Task: Read the poem with your child and discuss possible movements and expression that they might use. For example you might talk about emphasising the words *clattered* and *clashed* to sound like an actual clatter and clash, or raising an imaginary hat when 'a French cocked hat' is mentioned.

Name	Date

Creating a scene

◼ Read the passage below taken from the end of 'The Highwayman'. What does it make you see in your imagination?

> And still on a winter's night, they say, when the wind is in the trees,
> When the moon is a ghostly galleon tossed upon cloudy seas,
> When the road is a gypsy's ribbon looping the purple moor,
> The highwayman comes riding—
> Riding—riding—
> The highwayman comes riding, up to the old inn-door.
>
> Over the cobbles he clatters and clangs in the dark inn-yard,
> He taps with his whip on the shutters, but all is locked and barred,
> He whistles a tune to the window, and who should be waiting there
> But the landlord's black-eyed daughter—
> Bess, the landlord's daughter—
> Plaiting a dark red love-knot into her long black hair.
>
> *Alfred Noyes*

◼ Highlight or underline the parts of the text (words or phrases) that help to set the scene in your imagination.

◼ In the space below, sketch some of the images the verses of the poem create in your imagination.

Poem © 1914, Alfred Noyes.

POETRY

Dear helper
Objective: To identify parts of a poem that help to set the scene.
Task: Read through the poem with your child then ask them to read it carefully to themselves, picking out words and phrases that help to set the scene or create a picture of the scene in their imagination.

Name	Date

The Mistletoe Bough

◼ Read the poem, then tell the story to your helper.

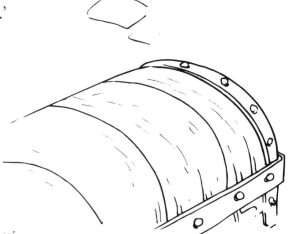

The mistletoe hung in the castle hall,
The holly branch shone on the old oak wall;
And the baron's retainers[1] were happy that day,
Keeping their Christmas holiday.
The baron saw with a father's pride
His beautiful child, young Lovell's bride;
While she with her bright eyes seemed to be
The star of the goodly company.

'I'm weary of dancing now,' she cried;
'Here wait a moment – I'll hide – I'll hide!
And, Lovell, be sure you are first to trace
The clue to my secret hiding place.'
Away she ran – and her friends began
Each tower to search, and each nook to scan;
And young Lovell cried, 'Oh where do you hide?
I'm lonely without you, my own dear bride.'

They search all night and they searched next day!
And they kept on searching 'til a week passed away!
In the highest, the lowest, the loneliest spot,
Young Lovell sought wildly – but found her not.
And years flew by, and their grief at last
Was told as a sorrowful tale long past,
And when Lovell appeared, the children cried,
'See! the old man weeps for his long lost bride.'

At length an oak chest, that had long lain hid,
Was found in the castle. They raised the lid –
And a skeleton form lay mouldering[2] there,
In the bridal wreath of that lady fair!
Oh! sad was her fate! – in playful jest
She hid from her lord in the old oak chest.
It closed with a click – and, dreadful doom,
The bride lay locked in her living tomb!

Thomas Haynes Bayley (slightly adapted)

[1]*retainers = servants and followers;* [2]*mouldering = rotting*

Illustrations © Phil Garner/Beehive Illustration.

Dear helper
Objective: To read a narrative poem and show understanding of the story.
Task: Share the reading of the poem with your child – for example, by taking verses in turn. Then help your child to retell the story in the poem. Discuss what happened and talk about similar incidents today, such as children who get trapped in abandoned fridges.

POETRY

Name	Date

Meg Merrilies

- Read this poem by John Keats.
- Underline all the descriptive words and phrases.
- Highlight the words that rhyme.

Old Meg she was a Gipsy,
And lived upon the Moors;
Her bed it was the brown heath turf,
And her house was out of doors.

Her apples were swart blackberries,
Her currants, pods o' broom;
Her wine was dew of the wild white rose
Her book a churchyard tomb.

Her Brothers were the craggy hills,
Her Sisters larchen trees;
Alone with her great family
She lived as she did please.

No breakfast had she many a morn,
No dinner many a noon,
And, 'stead of supper, she would stare
Full hard against the moon.

But every morn, of woodbine fresh
She made her garlanding,
And, every night, the dark glen Yew
She wove, and she would sing.

And with her fingers, old and brown,
She plaited Mats o' Rushes,
And gave them to the cottagers
She met among the bushes.

Old Meg was brave as Margaret Queen
And tall as Amazon;
An old red blanket cloak she wore,
A chip hat had she on.
God rest her aged bones somewhere!
She died full long agone!

John Keats

POETRY

Illustrations © Phil Garner/Beehive Illustration.

Dear helper
Objective: To read a poem by a major poet.
Task: Read this poem taking verses in turn. Discuss any archaic and unfamiliar vocabulary. Help your
child to pick out descriptive words and phrases and identify rhyming words.

All in a good clause (3)

Noun clauses act like **nouns**. They are usually introduced by the following connectives: **that**, **whether**, **who**, **whoever**, **whose**, **where**, **why**.

◼ Choose suitable **relative pronouns** (connectives) to link the **main clauses** and **noun clauses**. The first one has been done for you.

Main clause	Connective (relative pronoun)	Noun clause
Zoe could not remember	what	the homework was.
No one knows		broke the window.
My teacher taught		hard work brings success.
I do not know		suitcase that is.
A film has been made about		dinosaurs could be cloned.
The weather man was not sure		it would rain.
Do not let strangers in		they might be.
I can tell you		a good mechanic can be found.
The bill should be paid by		caused the accident.
Tim told the teacher		he couldn't do the work.

Illustrations © Phil Garner/Beehive Illustration

Dear helper
Objective: To investigate clauses by understanding how they are connected.
Task: Though the terminology is difficult, the task is quite easy. Don't worry if your child doesn't immediately start to use the correct terminology. Ask your child to read the two clauses and try out different connectives until they find one which sounds right. Sometimes, either of two connectives works equally well.

Name	Date

The Rain-Making Ceremony

For the Lango people of Uganda, rain is a matter of life and death. Every year, they perform this ceremony to make sure that the rains come.

◼ Read 'The Rain-Making Ceremony', but be careful – if you read it too well, it might work!

Verse	Response
We overcome this wind.	We overcome.
We desire the rain to fall, that it be poured in showers quickly.	Be poured.
Ah! rain, I beg you to fall. If you rain, it is good.	It is good.
A drizzling confusion.	Confusion.
If it rains and our food ripens, it is good.	It is good
If the children rejoice, it is good.	It is good.
If it rains, it is good. If our women rejoice, it is good.	It is good.
If the young men sing, it is good.	It is good.
A drizzling confusion.	Confusion.
If our grain ripens, it is good.	It is good.
If our women rejoice.	It is good.
If the children rejoice.	It is good.
If the young men sing.	It is good.
If the aged rejoice.	It is good.
An overflowing in the granary.	Overflowing.
May our grain fill the granaries.	May it fill.
A torrent in flow.	A torrent.
If the wind veers to the south, it is good.	It is good.
If the rain veers to the south, it is good.	It is good.
Ah! rain, I beg you to fall.	Fall! Fall!

The Lango People, Uganda

◼ Discuss why rain is so important to the Lango people.

POETRY

Dear helper
Objective: To read a text from a different culture.
Task: Share the reading of this ceremony with your child. Take it in turns to read the verse and response. Think of actions to go with the ceremony. Discuss the importance of rain to the Lango people.

Name   Date

My Dad, Your Dad

📣 Read this dialogue poem aloud. It would be best to read it with someone else, but you could also read it by yourself, using two different voices.

My Dad, Your Dad
My dad's fatter than your dad,
Yes, my dad's fatter than yours:
If he eats any more he won't fit in the house,
He'll have to live out of doors.

Yes, but my dad's balder than your dad,
Yes, my dad's balder, O.K.,
He's only got two hairs left on his head
And both are turning grey.

Ah, but my dad's thicker than your dad,
My dad's thicker, alright.
He has to look at his watch to see
If it's noon or the middle of the night.

Yes, but my dad's more boring than your dad.
If he ever starts counting sheep
When he can't get to sleep at night, he finds
It's the sheep that go to sleep.

But my dad doesn't mind your dad.
Mine quite likes yours too.
I suppose *they* don't always think much of US!
That's true, I suppose, that's true.

Kit Wright

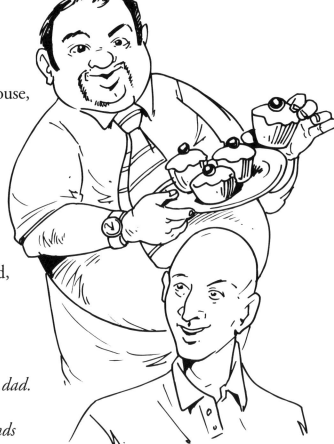

📣 Write your own dialogue poem based on an everyday conversation. It doesn't have to rhyme. Prepare it for performance.

Poem © 1978, Kit Wright; illustrations © Phil Garner/Beehive Illustration.

Dear helper
Objective: To use a performance poem as a model for own writing.
Task: Read the poem with your child, each taking a part. Encourage as much expression as possible. Discuss what everyday conversation might be used to write a similar poem. Improvise the conversation to help with the writing.

Name	Date

Onomatopoeia

Some words suggest the sound they describe. This effect is called **onomatopoeia**. Here are some examples:

■ Try to think of more examples and write them on the back of this sheet.

■ **Onomatopoeic** words can be used together so that the sound of the paragraph or poem reflects its meaning. Read this onomatopoeic poem, then write your own, using words from the examples above. Use the back of this sheet or a separate piece of paper.

> Plip, plop, rain drop
> Drip, drop, drizzle.
> Splatter, patter, plip, plop,
> Miserable mist and mizzle.
>
> Pitter, patter raindrops
> Splash, plash, plonk, plink,
> Dropping on my window panes
> Like water dripping in a sink.

POETRY

Dear helper
Objective: To explore onomatopoeia.
Task: The term *onomatopoeia* (pronounced *on-o-mah-ta-pee-a*) is quite difficult to remember and spell, but the concept is easy – and fun. Take it in turns to say the words in a way that emphasises their sound. Talk about creatures, places and situations where each word might be used. Help your child to develop one of the ideas into a poem.

www.scholastic.co.uk

◼SCHOLASTIC

Also available in this series:

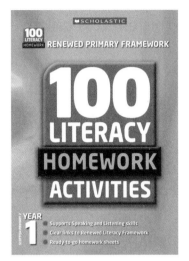

ISBN 978-1407-10115-6

ISBN 978-1407-10116-3

ISBN 978-1407-10117-0

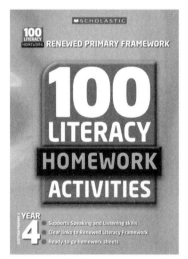

ISBN 978-1407-10118-7

ISBN 978-1407-10119-4

ISBN 978-1407-10120-0

To find out more, call: 0845 603 9091
or visit our website www.scholastic.co.uk